Distant Indigo
CLARA MASON FOX
PIONEER, PAINTER, POET *of* ORANGE COUNTY, CALIFORNIA

LORRAINE PASSERO

Copyright © 2017 by Lorraine Passero
Second Edition

All rights reserved. No part of this publication may be reproduced, stored in a retrieval system, or transmitted, in any form or by any means, electronic, mechanical, photocopying, recording, or otherwise, without the prior written permission of the author.

ISBN-13: 978-0-9849504-3-0
LCCN: 2013901767

Printed in the United States of America

Design and Typography by Craig Lockwood and Michael McCullen

Pacific-Noir Press
www.Pacific-Noir.com
1278 Glenneyre St.
Laguna Beach, CA 92651

This is dedicated to the one I love—Jon

CONTENTS

Chapter One 7

Chapter Two 11

Chapter Three 15

Chapter Four 19

Chapter Five 23

Chapter Six 27

Chapter Seven 31

Chapter Eight 37

Chapter Nine 41

Chapter Ten 45

Chapter Eleven 49

Chapter Twelve 53

Chapter Thirteen 57

Chapter Fourteen 61

Chapter Fifteen 63

Chapter Sixteen 69

Chapter Seventeen 73

Chapter Eighteen 77

Chapter Nineteen 81

Chapter Twenty 85

Chapter Twenty-One 87

Chapter Twenty-Two 93

Chapter Twenty-Three 97

Chapter Twenty-Four 101

Chapter Twenty-Five 105

Chapter Twenty-Six 109

Chapter Twenty-Seven 113

Chapter Twenty-Eight 117

Chapter Twenty-Nine 123

Chapter Thirty 127

Chapter Thirty-One 135

Chapter Thirty-Two 139

Chapter Thirty-Three 143

Chapter Thirty-Four 145

Chapter Thirty-Five 149

Chapter Thirty-Six 153

Chapter Thirty-Seven 157

Chapter Thirty-Eight 161

Chapter Thirty-Nine 165

Chapter Forty 169

Chapter Forty-One 175

Poems From
   "In Pleasant Places" 181

Resources/Index 186/188

ACKNOWLEDGMENTS

I have a wonderful team of people to thank. Each one of them guided me and offered their enthusiastic support while writing this book.

Rochelle Mancini and Janet Whitcomb are two talented women who checked the facts and carefully edited the first manuscript. Craig Lockwood and Michael McCullen of Laguna Beach's Pacific-Noir Press helped to polish the second edition to make the book more brilliant through their editing and artistic skills. Both are experienced and extraordinarily talented people.

Orange County historian Phil Brigandi and Assistant Archivist Chris Jepsen from the Orange County Archives assisted me in navigating through extensive records to find the detailed information I needed for historic accuracy.

Cooper Union Archives Librarian Carol Salomon through her research provided me with historical documents from the Cooper Union Archives Department.

Clara Mason Fox's niece, Gwen and her husband Boyd Johnson willingly took time to share stories of their Aunt Clara, through e-mails, phone calls, and during a visit to Colorado.

Lucille Cruz is more than Silverado's librarian; she is the canyon's local historian who directed me to many of the sources used during the course of my research.

Marian Norris from Heritage Hill Historical Park in Lake Forest was invaluable in tracking down information and pictures of old El Toro.

I am appreciative of my family and friends for their encouragement throughout my writing process.

I especially want to thank my husband Jon, not only for his ancestry of artistic and creative people, but also for cooking dinner on numerous occasions while I was busy typing and conducting online research.

Lastly, I am grateful to Clara Mason Fox, and to her niece, Marge Seeman, for having the foresight to preserve artwork, family photos, and letters for future generations to discover and appreciate.

CHAPTER ONE

Opening the back door and stepping into the kitchen of my husband Jon's grandmother Marge's wonderful old 1920s Craftsman bungalow on Glenneyre Street in Laguna Beach, California, was always a special experience.

For me, it was like holding a seashell to my ear, closing my eyes and listening quietly—and then hearing the sound of the ocean inside faintly whispering.

This house-by-the-sea with weathered shingles and small-paned windows was now like an empty shell.

Walking through the doorway I imagined how many memories the old place's walls must hold.

Grandma Marge had lived in the cozy seaside bungalow since 1925, the year it was built, and she had continued to stay there alone, for many long years after her husband Ed Seeman died.

But we didn't know what a treasure-trove of family memories we would find until Grandma Marge passed away, and we had to clean out the house.

We stood in the kitchen for a few minutes, recalling how many times we'd gathered around the old round wooden kitchen table, feasting on Grandma's pot roast and gravy while sharing stories.

With winter's chilling ocean winds blustering outside, the fire crackling and snapping in the fireplace gave us warmth and comfort. Nearby, in a small rocking chair that had seemed just right for her petite frame, Grandma Marge occasionally added pieces of fragrant Eucalyptus wood to keep the fire going.

Summertime meant bright sunny days at the beach, just a short walk across Pacific Coast Highway and down the cliff. Returning from the beach exhausted and hungry from swimming, we would hurriedly rinse the sand from our feet with icy cold water from the hose next to Grandma Marge's back door before entering though the kitchen.

Something tasty, perhaps a plate of oatmeal and raisin cookies, or thick slices of homemade bread and strawberry jam, could always be found on the kitchen counter.

Now, without Grandma Marge the house had a different feeling—lifeless, as quiet as a classroom after the students have gone home on the last day of school.

We stood there for a few moments and Jon looked at me. His glance brought me back to the reality of our visit. The house needed to be cleaned out. Starting with the first floor, we cleared away the furnishings and removed dusty paintings of wildflowers and desert landscapes.

TATTERED CURTAINS—A DUSTY BOX

Together, we climbed the worn, creaky wooden staircase and entered a low-roofed attic room where tattered curtains filtered light through the window. Faded pink wallpaper with a tiny floral pattern covered the walls.

"Jon," I asked, looking around, "how many years do you suppose have gone by since anyone had even bothered to go *into* this part of the house?"

Jon shrugged.

At first, we saw only the expected objects found in a room used for storage: long-forgotten pieces of broken furniture, piles of discarded clothing, and stacks of books.

But hidden away in a dim corner, an old box caught my eye.

Wondering what the neglected carton might contain, I knelt down, shook loose a cloud of dust that settled like a mist around me, and pried open the lid.

Stacked neatly inside were several small sketchbooks with old-fashioned covers. Next to them was a collection of letters, handwritten in pen and ink that had faded from black to faint gray.

Then, in a packet carefully tied with string, I found pages of poetry, along with black and white photographs.

While Jon and his family members were busy cleaning, I sat transfixed, swept back across the gulf of years into a time and place where my husband's Grandma Marge had spent so much of her life.

Leafing through the brittle, cream-colored pages of the sketchbooks, I was amazed. Who had created these precisely detailed pencil drawings of sunbathers and beach-goers dressed in long swimming outfits?

Beach scenes crowded the surface of the paper, as if not to waste any available space on the page. Blowing away another cloud of dust uncovered a mysterious scrawl on the cover of the sketchbook.

Clara L. Mason, August 1894
(Arch Beach)

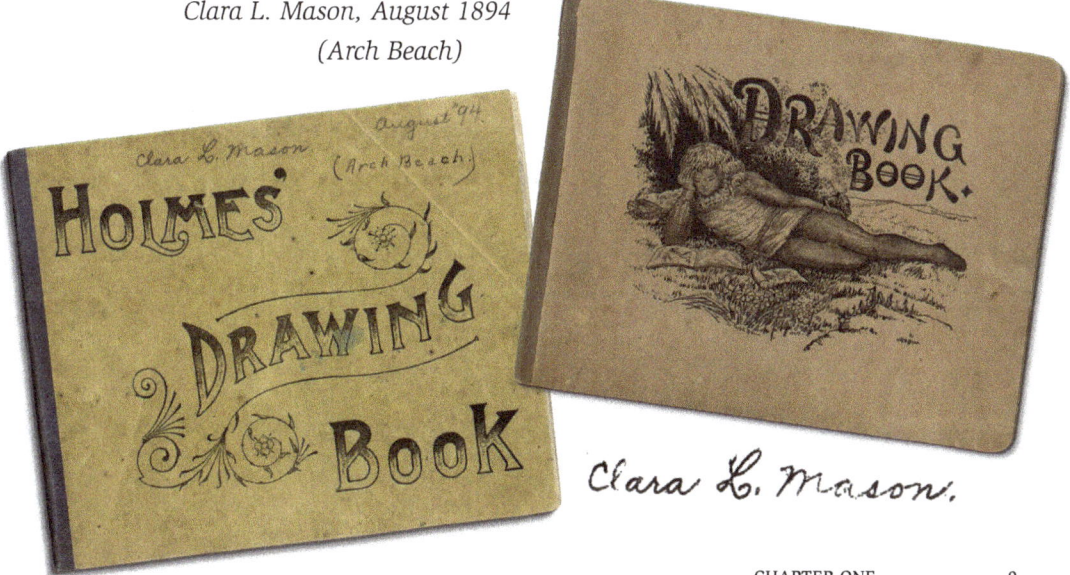

CHAPTER TWO.

*ifting through her drawings and writings in that time-forgotten room, my curiosity grew.*

This was like a *Nancy Drew* mystery!
And the mystery was *"Who was Clara Mason?"*

Why had her drawings, letters and poetry been saved in this attic for so many years? Whatever the reason—I felt compelled to find the answers.

A LINK TO THE PAST

Before she died Grandma Marge had given my husband Jon a wonderful family heirloom. This little rocking chair with a green velvet seat had always seemed to reach out across Time to connect us with the past.

For years I'd rocked our daughter Inaeko to sleep in that comfortable chair I loved so much. Now, leafing through the pages of Clara's sketchbook I saw a sketch of Clara's own mother—sitting in the very same chair.

My attention focused on that drawing, and for a few silent moments I experienced—in a way I can't easily explain—an eerie feeling that I would be sharing more connections with Clara.

After leaving Grandma's Marge's house that day I began searching, hoping to find out more about her.

What I soon discovered was our first connection—our love of drawing.

But there was more. We both had been schoolteachers.

Then, a few days later, reading through another bundle of letters, I found out that Clara had journeyed alone—all the way from California to the East Coast to study at New York City's famed school of art, Cooper Union.

CONNECTING WITH CLARA

New York City?

Another connection. New York is where I'd grown up. I couldn't help identifying more and more with Clara.

She had made a nearly three-thousand-mile journey across an America of only forty-three States! Arizona and New Mexico, were territories. Hawaii and Alaska wouldn't become states for more than another half-century.

This had taken Clara, still a young woman, almost a week of travel by rail. It's a long-enough trip to take today, flying by plane, but then, it was an adventure.

CLARA'S TIME

Living at the end of the nineteenth century, during the late 1800s—in what today we call *"The Victorian Era,"* women were expected to stay home, take care of the family, and do the household chores. But Clara had achieved much more than most young women living during those times.

I realized that not only had I opened this box, but the box had magically opened a window in Time through which I could look and learn about this remarkable woman and the beautiful little town where she, and now I, lived.

We finished our work that day, but instead of just walking away and leaving behind discarded old stuff, I'd come away with a real treasure.

WORD SPREADS

Hearing of my interest in Clara Mason, other members of the family soon came forward.

"Did you know," revealed one of Jon's relatives "I have copy of a book Clara had owned, *Great Expectations,* written by the famous nineteenth century author Charles Dickens? Take a look," she said, handing it to me.

Opening this old volume I immediately recognized inscriptions made on the pages margins, little notes in Clara's tidy cursive handwriting.

ANOTHER MYSTERY TO SOLVE

I quickly decided I needed an expert's help.

Bundling up the sketchbooks I paid a visit to the Laguna Beach Art Museum. The museum's curator was amazed.

"The earliest artwork we've collected dates from the early nineteen hundreds. These sketches of Clara's drawings are dated eighteen ninety-four. This is really exciting, Lorraine, I'd very much like to display Clara's sketches in the museum. Do you know if there is anything else beside the letters and sketchbook you discovered in the attic?"

175. 1796 Glenneyre   1925-35 (E)

A Craftsman house with box plan, multi-gabled roof and shingle siding. A front-facing gable emerges out of main roof; a lean-to overhang forms the small entry porch. Entry is elevated and reached via concrete steps. Multi-paned windows adorn the south corner. An ocean stone retaining wall extends across the front of the lot. These same stones are used to form meandering pathways that form a lovely garden connecting the house with the garage in the rear.

Originally and still owned by Marguerite Seeman (he has since passed away). He was a miner in the Mohave and left it to come to Laguna Beach in 1919. His first job locally was in Dana Point doing stone layout for the Scenic Inn and park; the stone work was like that which adorns the house today and, in fact, the stones he used on his house were brought up from his job in Dana Point. He opened the El Arco garage and gas station at 1793 South Coast Highway subsequent to his employment in Dana Point. Those Mediterranean Revival buildings which formed the El Arco garage still stand today. ==The house was designed by Marguerite's aunt, Clara Mason Fox, artist and author of history on El Toro.==

CHAPTER THREE

*W**as there anything else? With my curiosity further heightened I began gathering more bits and pieces about young Clara Mason's life. After talking to family members I learned Clara was my husband's great-great aunt.*

Soon I was visiting the Orange County Archives, various libraries, and Heritage Hill Historical Park—where there is so much to learn about Orange County's rich history from census information, and reading newspaper and magazine stories from the past.

More details of Clara's life surfaced. For example, while visiting the City of Laguna Beach's Building Department to discover the history of Grandma Marge's house, I came across an interesting document that stated that the house was designed by her niece—our Clara Mason—who had written the history of El Toro.

"...the history of El Toro..."

That sentence opened yet another door, and another pathway to follow.

More new information—and questions—unfolded when I visited the library staffed by the Saddleback Area Historical Society.

Going through their files I found photos of the very places Clara had drawn in her sketchbooks.

A LADY AND A SCHOLAR

I learned that Clara Mason was considered a scholarly lady, held in such high esteem by the local Women's Club that its members had asked her to write a history of their town, El Toro.

In addition to unearthing and studying documents, I had the chance to find out about Clara's life by talking to people who were still alive and had personally known her and recognized her talents as an artist and writer.

Clara began slipping out of History's dusty pages to reveal herself to me in a very special way.

It was as if she wanted me to tell her story.

There were moments when I felt as though she was guiding me to people and places providing additional answers about who she was.

Across a gap of seventy-five years, Clara's insights about nature, history, the things she most valued in life, became increasingly clear. Looking again and again at her drawings and reading her El Toro history and poetry, I saw through her eyes what was important to her.

Clara's sketches, letters, poetry—creative graphic and written forms of expression from the nineteenth and early twentieth centuries—provided an understanding of her life and the times in which she lived much better than any history book could. Holding this "history" in my hands was as if I was holding something alive.

With each additional discovery I found myself wondering: How many other boxes lie forgotten in attics, basements, on shelves in closets, waiting to be discovered—waiting to tell their story? Waiting to make someone's life part of the rich tapestry of our history?

CHAPTER FOUR

lara Mason was born in Jackson Township, Ohio, on November 24, 1873, eight years after the Civil War ended.

Her father, George Mason, was a veteran who'd served in an Ohio Volunteer Regiment, fighting for the North.

Northerners were opposed to slavery and wanted the United States to remain united as one country. The Southerners, who profited from slave labor, were willing to become a separate country to keep slavery legal.

A BITTER CONFLICT

So bitter had that conflict become during that devastating period that families were torn apart. Then, as now, people moved around, and many stories from the time tell of how a man living in the North, might find himself fighting against his own brother or a family member, living in a Southern state.

When the war ended in 1865, though the nation remained united, many new problems faced America. During the war more crops than usual were needed to feed soldiers on both sides.

Farmers had borrowed money to buy farm equipment and supplies to meet the crop demand.

With the war's ending, however, so did the demand for increased food production. Farmers were left in debt, and with farms and ranches forming much of the United States, our economy suffered.

Clara's parents, Nancy and George Mason, were one of Ohio's many farming families struggling to pay the debts they owed.

The Masons were typical of many Americans during that time. Hard-working, self-sufficient people, they were used to growing enough food to feed their family through difficult economic times. The Mason children soon learned about responsibility and the importance of caring for each other to survive. Clara was the youngest of the three children, the oldest being her brother Charley, and sister Nellie.

LIVING IN THE 1870S

For a young person, especially a girl living on a farm during the eighteen hundreds, life was very different.

Today, kids complain about chores such as loading the dishwasher or taking out the trash. But for the Mason children—Clara, her older brother Charley and older sister, Nellie—farm life offered many challenges.

Farms were often a distance from one another, so families were isolated. Stores and neighbors could be miles away, and doctors were rarely nearby. Being self-sufficient meant the growing crops and both raising and hunting animals for food. Any extra, or "surplus," food was stored for winter or sold at market. The Masons also bartered by exchanging some of their surplus for items they needed.

DAY-BY-DAY, SEASON-BY-SEASON

Farmers such as the Masons lived day-by-day, according to the seasons.

Fall and winter months meant facing storms, harsh winds, and rain.

Spring was welcomed with its mild weather when budding plants popped through the thawing ground.

Summer brought hot winds, harsh sun, and long hours of work planting. During the summer Clara could look out of her bedroom window and see row after row of toast-colored wheat stalks and the bright green stems, with yellow tassels of corn growing in their field.

With summer's end came the fall harvesting.

Autumn meant it was time for the fattened pigs to be slaughtered. Meat was then salt-cured or smoked to last through the winter months. Men and boys hunted, and the crack of gunshots rang through the golden fields as wild turkeys and migrating ducks provided another source of food in the fall.

Winter arrived with a fierce cold snap in 1873, the year Clara was born. Record-breaking temperatures dropped as low as minus two degrees. Freezing rain and ice glazed the houses, wooden barns, and dirt roads. Snow and high winds forced the Mason children to stay indoors for days.

Clara and the other Mason children were expected to entertain themselves by playing with handmade dolls or a game of ball and jacks. Reading or drawing pictures by the light of a kerosene lantern were favorite pastimes as well.

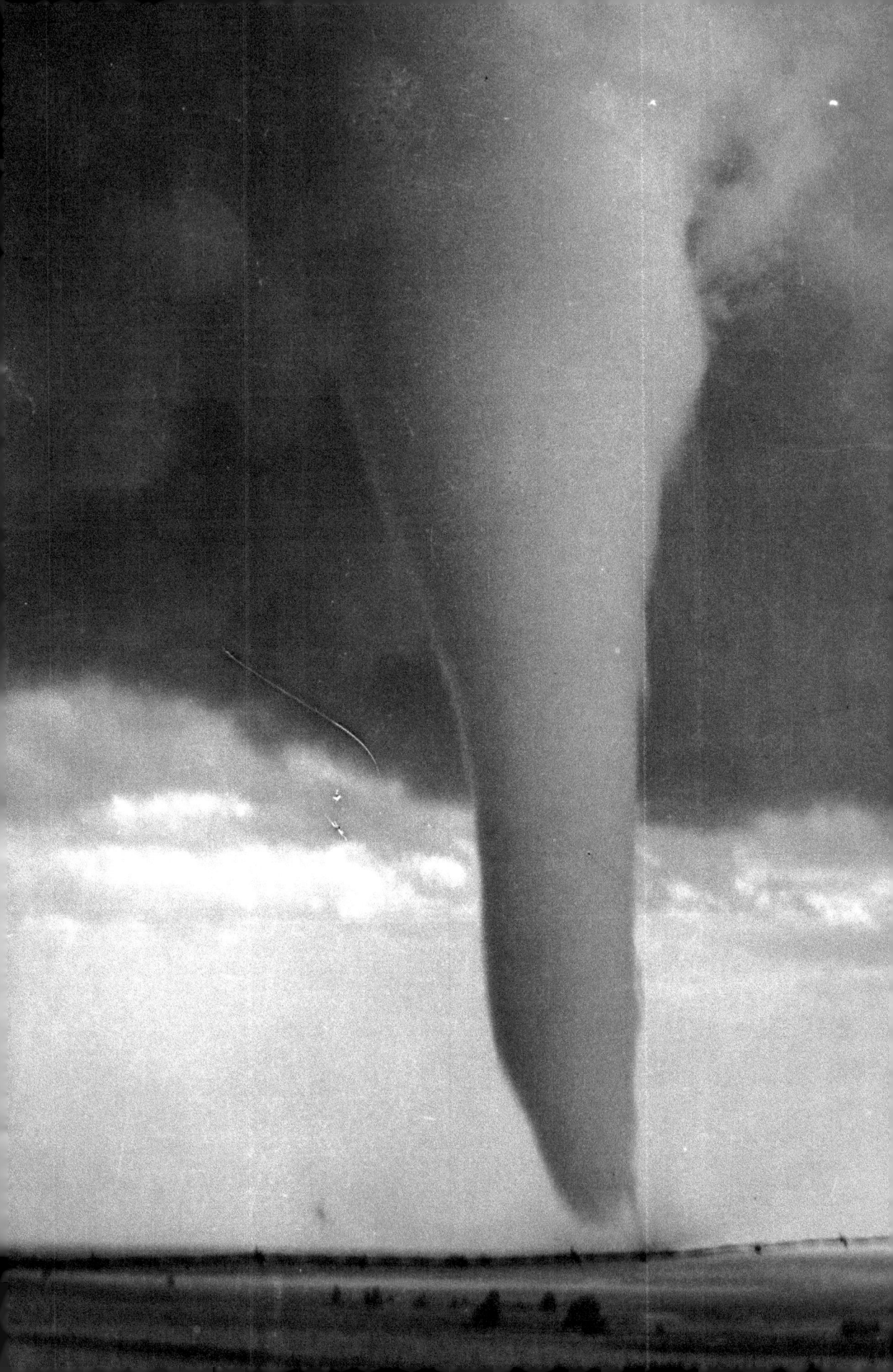

CHAPTER FIVE

Staying busy might have distracted the young Masons from the fearful possibility of another kind of dangerous storm touching down and destroying their house—*tornadoes*.

Today, we can analyze data from hundreds of weather stations and use computer modeling to predict and warn about the potential of tornadoes. At that time, however, a severe thunderstorm was the only warning sign of a possible tornado's arising.

KEEPING A "WEATHER EYE"

This meant paying attention to environmental conditions and keeping a very careful eye on the weather.

Then as now, most tornadoes occurred in the late afternoon or early evening during the spring and summer months. Fierce winds caused roofs to be torn from homes, valuable livestock such as horses and cows, snatched away suddenly by the wind, would simply disappear. Trees were uprooted and blown for miles only to topple onto houses, forcing everyone to take shelter in cellars until the tornado passed.

Still, rain, snow, or extreme temperatures, tasks around the farm had to be done.

Chores were a necessary part of their day, beginning at four, every morning. Except during times of disaster, little Clara was expected, even at her very young age, to do her share of the farm work along with Charley, who was nine years older, and Nellie who was older by three years.

MEALTIME AT THE MASON FARM

For breakfast, Clara and her family did not go to the nearest fast-food drive-thru for a breakfast egg sandwich—there were no fast-food restaurants. So, instead, the children went to their barn each morning ro gather fresh, still-warm eggs from the chickens.

As they came back to the farmhouse, smells of sweet corn muffins or freshly baked bread met them. Grains used by Mrs.

Mason to make these baked goods had come directly from the Mason's fields and were ground into flour at the local mill.

Inside the warm kitchen, hot pans were carefully removed from a wood-burning oven. After eating breakfast—by candlelight during dark mornings—the low mooing of cows meant they needed to be milked. Back to the barn the youngsters went.

BACK TO WORK

After they finished, the warm fresh milk they'd collected in pails was then poured into large metal cans.

With the cows milked, clucking chickens demanded to be fed. Next, the farm's hard-working horses needed brushing and grooming.

Even in the frost of winter the snow-covered barn that housed the animals' stalls had to be cleaned.

But work didn't stop there, and without electricity or any technology, farm work never really stopped at all. Then, as now, farm work is hard on clothes, which get dirty very quickly.

Oct. 10, 1895

CHAPTER SIX

Without electric washers or gas dryers, washing clothes meant scrubbing them by hand on a washboard in a big tub, then hanging them to dry on a clothesline with clothespins to keep them from blowing away. Because of this, work-clothes soon wore out. Time was then taken to mend all the family's garments, sewing one careful stitch at a time.

CARING FOR CLOTHING

Torn shirts, pants, and dresses were either patched or mended with a pair of scissors, needle, and thread. Young girls were judged by how neatly they could sew a seam or make a torn shirt look if not "good as new" then, "good enough." This way clothing was able to last for several years.

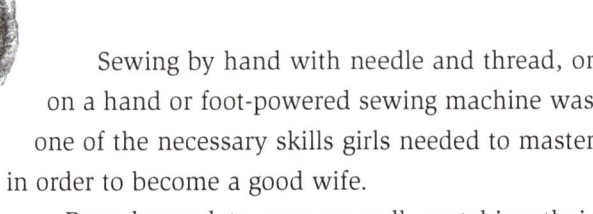

Sewing by hand with needle and thread, or on a hand or foot-powered sewing machine was one of the necessary skills girls needed to master in order to become a good wife.

Boys learned to sew as well, watching their fathers or uncles repair the horse's bridles and harnesses.

HUNTING FOR SMALL GAME

Fathers and uncles also carefully taught sons and nephews the safe use of firearms and how shoot in order to hunt squirrels, rabbits, and other small game for meat. Later, they would learn to hunt deer.

Clara's brother Charley was expected to skin the animals, then hang the meat in the cool barn until it was ready to be cooked. Roasted chicken for dinner came from the Mason chicken coop. Clara might well have known the name of the chicken whose drumsticks she had for dinner that night!

BIGGER WORRIES

But there were bigger concerns than just washing clothes and cooking.

Farmers such as Clara's father had to worry about things that affected their families. How much food would they grow? Would there be enough rain? Would the soil be rich enough to grow the season's food for the family? Would insects or birds destroy the harvest?

And finally, would there be enough left to sell as cash crops for a good price?

CHAPTER SEVEN

In photographic images we see young Clara snuggled by her father's side during the mid-1870s. While knowing just when she lived by her face alone might not be possible, the clothing she and her father wear clearly tells us this was another century.

Clara's checkered dress would have been pressed with a heavy iron that had been heated in the fireplace or on the wood-burning stove in the kitchen.

Before this picture was taken, Clara's face would have been washed by her mother using water, hand-pumped from the farm's well into a bucket, carried to the house, and heated in a boiler on the wood-burning stove. There were no faucets or running water in the Mason's farmhouse.

SEEING THROUGH CLARA'S EYES

In 1880, Clara was seven years old. She had never seen TV or a movie, or heard a radio, or CD. They didn't exist. There were no computers, no mobile phones, no texts, or e-mail. The telephone—only recently invented—was not yet widely used.

Important communication was sent by telegraph and handwritten letters. While traveling a hundred miles on a train in 1880 might take five hours, the same trip on horseback, or in a horse-drawn buggy or carriage could take days, depending on the weather.

THROUGH THE CAMERA'S LENS, AN EVEN CLOSER LOOK

Photographs, however, did exist, and this image of the Mason family—all staring solemnly at the camera as they pose for their family portrait—was taken in Illinois.

Making such a memento was a big occasion in those days. Photography was costly and expensive. Long before the days of phone cameras, the family would make an appointment with a professional photography studio in town, a studio equipped with elaborate props such as carpets, statues, and elegant furniture.

For their part, the Masons would have dressed in their best clothes.

And, as cameras and the process of photography was very slow at this time, the photographer would have told everyone that they had to remain very still.

This was serious business, and the family, holding their breath, remained in the same position without squirming in front of the camera for some time—in order for the image to be "exposed."

Next, the image, now captured on a thin, light-sensitive glass plate in the camera, was removed and "fixed" with chemicals and finally "developed" and then "printed" on special silver-coated photographic paper.

DETAILS DEFINE THE DATE

The Mason children's clothing is identical to their parents' outfits. For this important event, Nellie might have carefully braided eight-year-old Clara's thick hair, then tied it in a ribbon. Although her lacy collar gives an impression of delicacy, it is in direct contrast to her scuffed shoes, worn from farm work. Nellie, the twelve-year-old "tween" with her hand on her dad's shoulder, has styled her hair like her mother's, neatly pulled back in a tight bun. Charley, at seventeen, looks like a grown man, standing dutifully behind his mother and little sister, Clara.

Closely observing details in a picture can be a doorway into another time.

DECORATIONS DEFINE DUTY

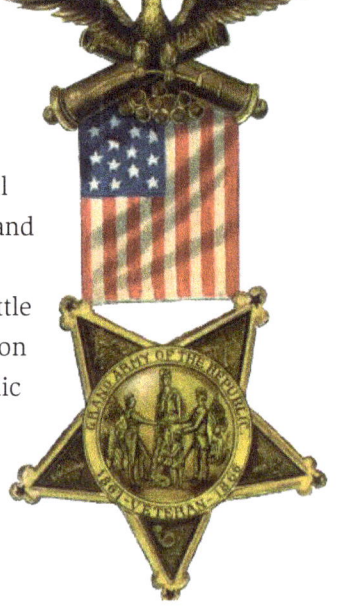

Clara's father, George Mason is wearing a medal on his jacket. From one small detail in the photograph, we now know that Clara's father served the Union Army during the Civil War, from 1860 to 1865, when the North and South fought against each other.

This military decoration, and the battle ribbon worn above it, identifies George Mason as a veteran of the Grand Army of the Republic (G.A.R.), an organization that assisted "Yankee" veterans after the war. It was the

forerunner of today's popular veterans' organizations such as the American Legion.

Researching George Mason's war records we learn that Clara's father was wounded in combat, receiving a gunshot injury to his left leg.

Clara's father also wears a gold chain which is attached to a pocket watch that we can't see because he has tucked into his vest as men did at that time.

In another photo, Clara is posing by herself. She looks serious, with a faraway look in her eyes.

CHAPTER EIGHT

 *lara's father and mother were determined to make a better life. The family decided to pack up and head West.*

Settling in Illinois, Clara's father continued to farm for the next few years. However, he was also a very skillful woodworker, and applying this additional skill he added to the family's income by building carriages. Since a horse-drawn carriage was as necessary as today's family car, this was definitely a useful second job.

Clara Mason was fourteen years old in 1887, when her parents decided once again to move, this time more than half a continent away to California—that amazing state bordering the Pacific Ocean, where gold and silver had been discovered and were there for the taking.

Perhaps she had heard her parents talking about the U.S. government's description of California as *"…hundreds of thousands of acres of the finest lands, blest with a climate equal to the fairest portions of Italy."*

CALIFORNIA DREAMING

Around the family dinner table Clara would certainly have heard her parents discussing "homesteading," which was a program allowing settlers to claim and receive free land by filing legal paperwork, living on the land for five years, and making improvements on the property.

Who knew better how to work the land than a family that had proven that they could, both in Ohio and in Illinois? So, when the Masons learned about land available for homesteading in Southern California's Orange County, they decided to pack their belongings and once again try to make a better life for themselves.

ALL ABOARD!

As the Masons boarded the train Clara must have felt both sad and excited. She was leaving all that was familiar, saying goodbye to family and friends with the understanding that she might not see some of them again.

Huffing and puffing the Atchison, Topeka, and Santa Fe Railway's big steam locomotive moved steadily across Illinois, to Kansas, then on to the Great Plains and Rocky Mountains, Surely the Mason family's anticipation as they looked from their train windows must have heightened their excitement.

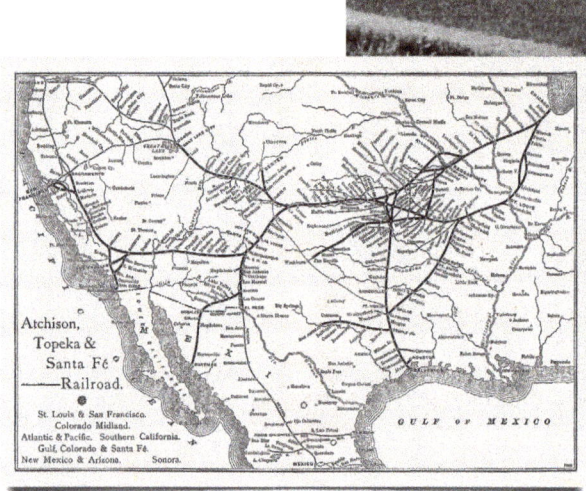

CHAPTER EIGHT

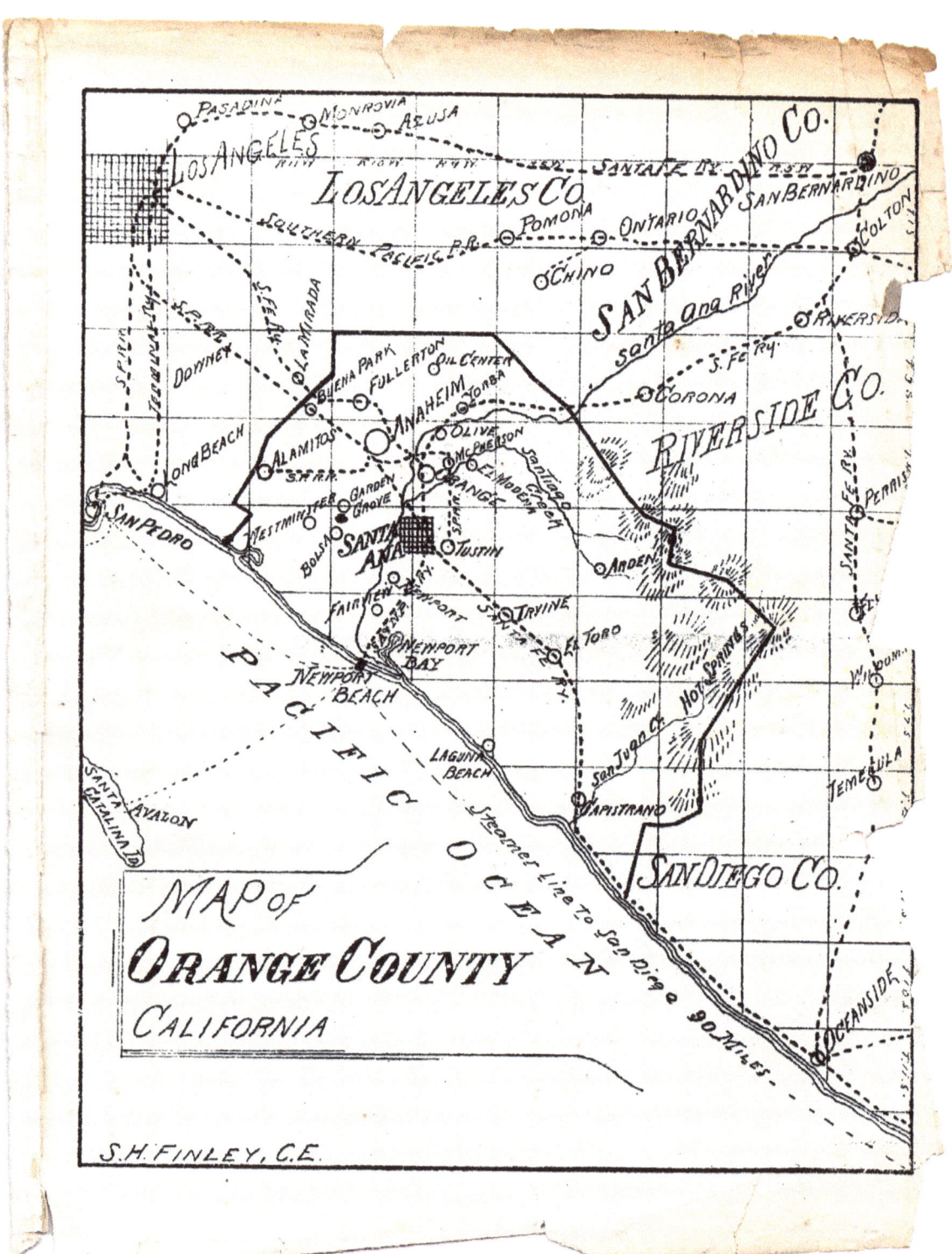

CHAPTER NINE

ailroad tracks from San Francisco recently had been extended south, beyond Los Angeles to San Diego.

Both the railroad and the government were encouraging settlers to move to Southern California. The time was right to claim land in or near one of the new towns being built along the railroad route. Surely it seemed like an appealing opportunity, especially for a bright teenager with big dreams.

None of Clara's letters or documents described the Mason's journey West, but long-distance transportation by railroad—where track existed—had replaced travel by horse, stagecoach, and wagon train. The Santa Fe Railroad first stretched into Orange County, California in 1887, the same year the Masons arrived.[1]

Official land records additionally reveal that after the Masons arrived in Orange County, they journeyed to Silverado Canyon, near the base of Saddleback Mountain, where they began homesteading on their land.

---

1. Other families had arrived before the Masons, but they'd traveled by covered wagon. The Foxes, Clara's soon to be in-laws, were just such a family; they had traveled to California in 1874, by wagon train.

HOME, SWEET-SMELLING HOME!

Much of this property was covered with white sage and fragrant wildflowers. What a contrast from the sparse, flat farmland of the Midwest. Silverado's crystal-clear streams cascading through this steep canyon were flanked with majestic sycamore and alder trees.

One story about the origins of the Masons' homestead goes like this: When a rich vein of silver ore was discovered more than three-hundred fortune seekers descended into the area that would become known as Silverado.

A stagecoach packed with prospectors arrived one day. The horses were given a break after the long journey, but it apparently wasn't enough for one poor horse named Buck. Buck, however, had had too much of stagecoach life and decided he would permanently rest in peace at that exact spot. "Buck's tree" became a known monument to the tired old horse who died beneath it on the Mason family's property.

CHAPTER TEN

Silverado Canyon might have been sunnier and warmer year-round than Illinois, but living there in the 1880s wasn't necessarily easier.

Once again the family needed to be self-reliant if they were going to endure the hardships and isolation of canyon life.

Dirt trails connected the canyon residents to a general store selling the crucial supplies that everyone needed. But it was some distance away, and flooding from heavy rains could make travel impossible.

When the "crick rose," no one could get in or out of the canyon. It would have been too dangerous to travel by horse and wagon.

BY THE BUCKETFUL

While there might be plenty of water outdoors, houses had no running water or flushing toilets, and the only bathrooms were outhouses. Without a well or a pump, one of Clara's jobs was to carry harsh-smelling, sulfur water from a spring about a quarter-mile away through the brush and back home.

But Silverado had many surprises, some of which could prove fatal.

SNAKES AND CRITTERS

A letter, written by Grandma Marge, told of one rainy day, when Clara, heading down to the creek, came across a big brown snake. Its markings looked exactly like the dried fern leaves she was walking through. Luckily, Clara had recently learned about the local plants and animals in school and from her own reading. She immediately recognized it as a rattlesnake whose poisonous venom might kill her.

Slowly backing up, she was able to make a quick getaway.

BEARS, BIG BIRDS AND BEASTS IN THE CANYON

Another family Silverado remembrance describes the wild animals that lived in the canyon, not only on the ground, but also in the air. Every mother knew she must keep a watchful eye over her children, even while doing daily chores such as washing dishes or sweeping the porch because grizzly bears and bobcats had been known to lurk nearby in search of food. Everyone in Silverado knew about the "big birds" that swooped down and carried away chickens, and some said "little children, too." Those "big birds" were California condors weighing up to twenty-five pounds with a wingspan of over nine feet. They constantly circled the canyons looking for prey.

PIONEER SOLUTIONS

Pioneers in Silverado Canyon needed to remain as responsive and capable of good judgment as a police officer on an emergency call.

One winter's evening, while Mr. Mason was away, Mrs. Mason—always on alert for strange happenings—heard noise coming from the chicken coop. The chickens were nervously clucking and flapping their wings.

Mrs. Mason warned Clara, Nellie, and Charley to stay in the house while she carefully picked up her shotgun and headed toward the coop to investigate the commotion. They did as they were told and sat close to the fireplace with its soft-glowing embers. Suddenly, a BANG resonated through the canyon.

Moments later their mother returned to the house—shivering not only from the cold, but also from what had just happened. A large stalking bobcat had been attempting to get into the chicken coop, and she had killed it.

BOBCAT SCARECROW

The next morning, Clara awakened at dawn to light a fire in the kitchen stove. The steep canyon walls were holding on tightly to the cold, and morning fog was moving slowly through the trees. Before beginning the day's chores, they looked near the side of the house. There was the dead bobcat, lying frozen on the ground, its fur matted on its lifeless body.

The family came up with an idea. Together, they dragged the bobcat's lean carcass to the side of the chicken coop and propped it up like a statue against the wall. For the next few days it served as a fine scarecrow, keeping other predators away from the chicken coop.

CHAPTER ELEVEN

ocated at one end of Silverado Canyon was a silver mine—while a coal mine, Carbondale, was on the other end.

In 1878, nine years before the Masons arrived, records show there were a number of stores, including two meat markets, offering necessities for the miners and other local residents.

At the meat markets, butchers cut fresh slabs of beef and pork for the miners' wives who stood in line on the sawdust-covered wooden floors, waiting their turn and exchanging the latest gossip.

Visiting engineers and investors had a place to stay at one of Silverado's three hotels. Horse-drawn carriages pulled up to the entrance where the hotel owner greeted them after their uncomfortable journey from as far away as Los Angeles.

In addition, two blacksmith shops were kept busy all hours of the day. Heat blasted from open flames softened the metal to be shaped into tools, machine parts, or horseshoes as the clanging of a hammer against an anvil added to the commotion. Most popular were the seven saloons serving whiskey and entertainment to the local miners. It was a lively time to live in the canyon.

END OF THE BOOM

By 1881, however, the silver and coal booms were coming to an end and many businesses had closed. The nearest city, Orange, was fourteen miles away. Santa Ana, the county seat, was a four-hour trip by horseback, and Anaheim was even further. By the time the Mason family began homesteading in 1887, the only signs of habitation to be found in the canyon were a few smoke-blackened stone chimneys where buildings, now burned, had once stood. Remaining were a few abandoned shacks, scattered on the hillsides.

SETTLING LAND CLAIMS

The Masons worked their acreage and legally filed their claim to the land.

In the early 1890s, the government began an investigation to identify homesteaders who were legally entitled to keep their ranches. The Masons and four other families were lucky enough to be granted full rights to their land.

The Sotos, a neighboring family, were not as fortunate.

Forty years earlier, in 1848, after losing the Mexican-American War, the Mexican government gave up claim to much of their land. Mexico signed the Treaty of Guadalupe Hidalgo, agreeing to give a good portion of their former territory, including California, to the United States.

A number of residents of Mexican and Native American descent were farmers in the canyons before the homesteaders arrived. The Sotos were one of these families.

This original Silverado Canyon family built a sturdy adobe home with a fireplace and lived there for many years. Because they had resided on this land for so long the Sotos believed the land was rightfully theirs and did not bother to file a claim. Eventually, the railroad purchased unclaimed land from the government and only the legal homesteaders were allowed to keep their property. So the Sotos los their home.

In contrast, the Masons prospered, building one home bigger than the next, until they finally owned one of the grandest homes in the canyon. Clara's early drawings offer an image of what their house looked like.

CHAPTER TWELVE

Around 1894, a hot sulfur spring was discovered on the Mason family property. People believed then, as many still do, that sulfur water is a cure for many health problems, from skin issues to stomach ailments. Word spread about the special find on their land. This gave the Masons a wonderful idea—they could open their property to the public with a pioneer spa.

SILVERADO SPA

At first people came to visit for the day. Those with ailments came to drink and soak in this miraculous water, as well as enjoy the natural beauty of Silverado Canyon.[2]

Eventually, because it was a long trip for visitors from Los Angeles and Long Beach and some of their guests wished to stay

---

[2]. "The Springs are becoming a favorite place for those suffering from throat or lung trouble..." Noted in *Silverado Sketches* (1957)

longer, the Masons expanded, offering overnight accommodations. Some visitors were local mining engineers. Others traveled a distance to hunt wild animals such as deer and grizzly bears, or to camp out and enjoy the natural surroundings.

STAYING IN THE NEWS

An article from a Santa Ana newspaper, *The Blade*, written around 1896, described a stay at *"Mason's Chateau"* where one could read and relax or simply enjoy the beautiful surroundings.

"...Lying full length under the shade of a sycamore tree with a volume of light literature, the air neither cold nor warm, yet so exhilarating, as only pure mountain air can be: the pleasant bubbling and splash of a running brook along the side and arched over which is growing the alder, birch and sycamore, through the openings, occasional glimpses of a sky of deep blue: nothing to do, nothing to think about, with no misgivings of duty unperformed...As the place becomes better known there is not the slightest doubt but that Mason's Springs will become one of the most popular resorts in the country."

Thanks to this newspaper review, we know *"Mason's Chateau"* had become Silverado Canyon's best-known luxury destination.

CHAPTER THIRTEEN

CHAPTER THIRTEEN

People living in Orange County's rural areas couldn't visit a mall, or shop at Nordstrom's, when they got tired of what they'd been wearing. Shopping meant leaving their family, spending long hours of travel on horseback or in a buggy or wagon, just to find a general store.

Instead, they would wear the same garments until they either grew out of them, or simply wore them until they could be worn no longer. *"Use up, wear out, make do or do without,"* went a common saying of those times.

FINDING FASHIONS

During the nineteenth century and into the beginning of the twentieth century, lacking fashion magazines or the Internet, the black and white pages of newspapers with an occasional photograph, or the *Saturday Evening Post* magazine were the only place a young woman in a rural community could find illustrations by artists such as Charles Dana Gibson of stylish women wearing the latest fashion trends from Paris. The "Gibson Girl" was the runway model of that time, celebrated for her feminine fashions and beauty.

However, unless they were very wealthy, many girls and their mothers sewed their own clothes, buying patterns and materials from mail-order catalogs featuring current fashions.

HAND-MADE AND CUSTOM FITTED

Since Clara's family could afford it, the dress she is wearing in this image may well have been custom-made by hand for her by a local dressmaker.

First, Clara's measurements would have been taken and written down for a perfect fit. The selected fabric would have been cut from a huge bolt of cloth and then laid out with the cloth matched to a pattern. Pieces were pinned or "basted" together and then put on a dressmaker's form where they could then be adjusted to assure the fit.

Careful work went into making the ruffles, pleats, and special trimming. Everything was then pressed by hand.

STEPPING OUT

Footwear, consisting of ankle-high leather street shoes, tended toward being sturdy and serviceable, but lacked the freedom of today's cushioned sneakers, stylish sandals, or cool flip flops.

CHAPTER FOURTEEN

In addition to her daily and unceasing round of chores, Clara attended school in the City of Orange several miles from home.

She was evolving into an intelligent young woman.

Clara loved to learn about her natural surroundings, and Silverado became her personal outdoor science camp. While walking the trails of their property she learned to identify the different kinds of minerals and rocks including speckled granite, white quartz, and amber-colored agates. She taught herself to recognize every kind of flower and tree that grew in the canyons, and knew both their popular and scientific names.

AN AVID READER

Those who knew Clara all agreed that throughout her life she was an avid reader who often gave books to children as presents.

Her sketchbooks reveal numerous pencil-sketches that portray people reading. But in the 1800s, few women had the vision of becoming more than a wife and mother. Both social traditions and custom held that "a woman's place was in the home."

Clara, however, was discovering that other options were available. Now, at nineteen, learned that her love of learning was also the pathway to a career.

CHAPTER FIFTEEN

In the late nineteenth century, most girls had no more than an eighth grade education and very few had the opportunity to go on to college. But if a young woman was smart, with high moral standards, she could become an elementary school teacher. Teachers, at that time did not need college-level training or a formal teaching credential.

This meant that teaching was a way for a single woman with a high school education but lacking a college degree to have a career.

Clara became one of the first, if not *the* first, teacher in Silverado Canyon. According to the canyon's librarian and local historian, Clara's classroom was a room at a ranch house where one of her students lived.

SADDLING UP FOR CLASSES

Before the days of cars and school buses, her students saddled up their horses and donkeys to ride on a dirt path to school. Even on wet and cold days students traveled miles to attend Miss Mason's class held in someone's parlor.

On warm days, students most likely moved outdoors on benches. Thirsty children needed to carry buckets of water from a nearby spring. No hall passes were required back then to get a drink of water—just dip a cup in the bucket!

Since very few school-aged children lived in the nearby canyons, both elementary school students and teenagers were grouped together to form a class. Children who had not yet learned to read would be in the same classroom as the older middle school students.

CLASS WORK

Spelling and grammar were taught as soon as a student was able to read. Practicing correct pronunciation meant students needed to read aloud before the class every day. Math problems and solutions were written on slate boards with chalk, and then erased to begin the next exercise.

Basic arithmetic techniques, including addition, subtraction and multiplication, much like today, were memorized and recited by rote.

Geography lessons consisted of memorizing, and reciting the locations of important rivers, mountain ranges, and places on a globe. Knowing the states, their capitals and important cities, were also required. Without computers everything needed to be handwritten and checked for errors.

PENMANSHIP WAS PREFERRED

Clear, readable cursive handwriting soon became a mark of the best of Clara's most promising students.

Writing was either by pencil or pen-and-ink, and writing with ink was an elaborate process. A pen with a steel-nib was first and carefully dipped into an inkwell. Then the student wrote until the ink began to run out. The pen was again dipped into the black or blue ink to continue writing. Excess ink was carefully soaked up from the paper with an ink blotter.

Spelling and grammar were checked in the dictionary. Correcting a mistake meant crossing out and a big blob of ink might be left on the paper. The teacher might have the student rewrite the entire exercise when that happened.

THEN, AS NOW

Among the students attending Clara's class were those from families who had mining claims nearby, as well as children of Mexican descent whose parents worked on local ranches. The students loved their young, pretty, and patient teacher. And Clara cared so much about her students that she learned Spanish to be able to communicate with those who couldn't speak English.

"Miss Clara," as her students called her, became so proficient that she wrote some of her poetry in Spanish. This verse is from one of her poems about Laguna Beach that was published in a newspaper.

> *!De nuevo la brisa salada sentir!*
> *De bondades quiero la una;*
> *Deseo volver y siempre vivir*
> *Acerca del mar en Laguna.*

> English Translation:
> *Oh, to feel once again the salt breeze*
> *o'er the foams*
> *Of joy, give me one, if no other!*
> *I want to return, and to dwell in a home*
> *By the sea in Laguna forever.*

Mi Deseo!

By CLARA MASON FOX.
(Written Specially for The Life.)

! Ay de mi! ! por las alas, por fuerza volar!
La cuadra ruidosa me molesta;
! Por in con las lomas al lado del mar
A' donde Laguna se acuesta!

El sol, tan oscuro de humo aqui,
Relumbra la playa Laguna;
Son de oro, ahoy, los penascos alli,
Son de plata debajo la luna.

La espuma se brilla, un tuerto liston;
Se caean las olas de verde,
Y cantan, ahora, y en el bajo son
El todo pesar se pierde.

! De nuevo la brisa salada sentir!
De bondades quiero la una;
Deseo volver y siempre vivir
Acerca del mar en Laguna.

(Editor's Note—A translation of this poem is printed below. The work is that of Mrs. Fox herself.)

MY DESIRE.

For wings and for powers to hasten,—ah, me!—
  From the noisy square to be flying!
To go with the hills that run down to the sea
  To where loved Laguna is lying.

The sun, so obscured by the smoke curtain here,
  Shines bright on the beach at Laguna;
The cliffs are of gold in his beams, I know, there;
  Are of silver 'neath glances of Luna.

The foam, a bright ribbon, in great loops is thrown
  On the sands; and the green waves are breaking;
They sing there, today, and in their deep tone
  All sorrow the heart is forsaking.

Oh, to feel once again the salt breeze o'er the foams
  Of joy, give me one, if no other!
I want to return, and to dwell in a home
  By the sea in Laguna, forever.

—TRANSLATED BY CLARA MASON FOX.

CHAPTER SIXTEEN

During that time, young women were required to remain unmarried while they were teaching. Dating and courting, however, were permissible.

In 1893, a young man, Theodore Payne, had recently emigrated from England to Orange County to study California's native plants and was living nearby. He soon landed a job as gardener for the famous actress Madame Helena Modjeska, who lived in the next canyon over from Silverado.

A SILVERADO ROMANCE?

In a book about his experiences in California, Theodore Payne quipped that a person might put on a clean shirt and overalls "...*to ride over the trail to Silverado Canyon to see the pretty young schoolteacher.*"[3]

3. Payne, Theodore. *Theodore Payne In His Own Words*. Pasadena, California: Many Moon Press, 2004

Could Theodore Payne have been making that trip to visit Clara? We may never know for sure if he was talking about himself but we *do* know they both shared a love and interest in plants indigenous to California, and both would contribute—Clara with her art and Theodore with his research and writings—to the knowledge we all share today.

And there was no other "pretty young schoolteacher" in Silverado Canyon.

A SILVERADO SEPARATION

While Clara was busy teaching, trouble was brewing at home.

Before Clara's parents married, Clara's mother Nancy had received a letter cautioning her about her husband-to-be, George.

Clara had saved it with the others in Grandma Marge's attic. It had been written by Nancy's brother, and sent from Camp Sherman, during the Civil War. He had known George for many years. Although no specific reason was given, he implied by noting that George was *"not the marrying kind and would not make a good husband."*

Nancy, however, was in love and married George in spite of the warning. And in the earlier years of their marriage, things seemed to work out, both in Ohio, where Nancy bore their three children, then later, when they moved to Illinois, the Masons had held together as a family.

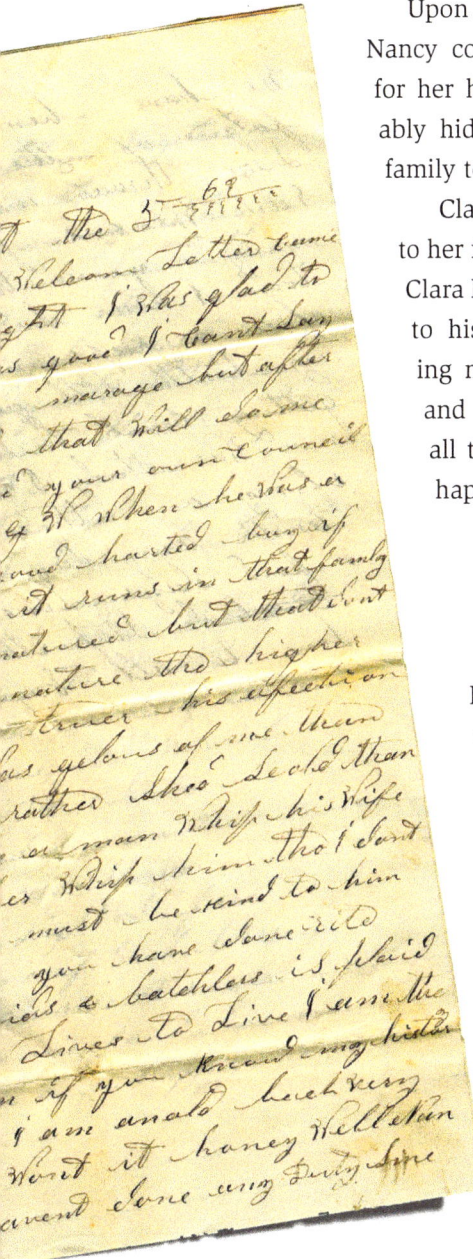

Upon moving to California and Silverado Canyon, Nancy continued to maintain a comfortable home for her husband and three children. She had probably hidden her sadness in an effort to keep the family together.

Clara loved her mother, but she was also close to her father. This is evident in the photos showing Clara leaning on his shoulder or holding on tightly to his sleeve. He was undeniably a hardworking man, laboring as a farmer, carriage maker, and businessman to provide his family with all the necessities. Yet he and Nancy were not happy together.

As a result, Clara's parents had drifted apart.

A SILVERADO DIVORCE

Divorce was uncommon in the nineteenth century but a telling clue was found by researching the County of Orange's Grant Deed records. These clearly show that the ownership of the Silverado Canyon property was listed in Mrs. Nancy Mason's name only.

This was uncommon in those times, when title to land holdings were usually held in the husband's name. What had happened between the couple is lost to history, but the result is clear.

Nancy and George had divorced.

CHAPTER SEVENTEEN

In May of 1897, with her husband gone, Clara's mother still had her children—now nearly all grown and still living with her. If George's support wasn't available, then Nancy—and her honey bees—would provide it.

From the following letter we can tell that Mrs. Mason not only took care of the Mason household by cooking, but she earned an income as well.

In the Canyon

My Dearest Clara,

I am on guard duty and have just been retrieved to go (make) a good dinner of lima beans, Swiss chard greens with lemon juice, bread and butter, homemade cheese, stewed dried peaches, and strawberries and cream, Tea and Jersey (cow) *milk.*

The bees make a lively hum and several hives seem to be on the very verge of sending forth swarms. I got one yesterday and had no trouble whatsoever with them. They were gentle fellows and took to their new home like a duck to water. I have to be constantly on the watch because the hum of work is so loud as to be confusing and sounds like a swarm issuing forth all the time.

-Mother

Sept. 7th, '95

THE BUZZ AROUND CHATEAU MASON

Nancy Mason proved very resourceful when it became necessary to financially support her family.

Like many of her neighbors, she decided to raise honeybees for income. This was a clever idea because sugar made from cane or beets was expensive and far less commonly used. With bees in abundance, honey was the readily available sweetener of choice.

Next to the house, Nancy Mason had erected an apiary, enclosures for the bees consisting of wooden crates where they could build their honeycombs. An extracting house—which stood beside the apiary—made it easy for the Masons to collect the sweet thick honey from the honeycombs.

A hand-crank spun the round extractor tank, where the honey separated from the combs and collected at the bottom.

Besides providing honey, bees served another important task, pollinating flowers on fruit trees. Honey comes in different flavors, depending on which flowers the bees pollinate. Because of this various types of honey can have an essence of lemon, orange, clover, or even blueberry.

Pollination from the bees ensured the Masons an abundance of fruit. In addition, marketing the amber-colored honey in Santa Ana proved to be a good business for Clara's mother. She sold the popular sweetener to stores and farm stands or bartered it in exchange for other needed items.

On a trip to Huntington Beach, Clara's mother *"...took some cans of honey—sold some and traded some for groceries (including two sacks of flour)."*

Experiencing her mother and father's divorcing was difficult for Clara.

CHAPTER EIGHTEEN

The idea of parents separating was something considered so shameful and unusual at that time that it wasn't openly discussed.

As a result, Clara developed strong feelings about the marriage commitment. She believed a couple, especially those with children, should try to work out their problems and stay together.

Clara's sister, Nellie, lived with her father for a few years after the Masons divorced. She met a fine gentleman, Neil McTaggart, who eventually would be elected in 1900 to the Orange City Council.

On March 6, 1889, *The Orange News* included among its announcements that "N.G. McTaggart, well and favorably known in Orange, will marry Nellie Mason of El Modena this evening at the home of her father, G.W. Mason."

In time, Neil and Nellie would have three children: Raymond, Ralph, and Marguerite, who was nicknamed "Marge."

FINDING THEIR OWN PATHS

Charley, Clara's beloved big brother, now worked far from home, but kept in touch through visits and letters. He held some unusual jobs, such as selling sheet music door-to-door and building booths for the annual Parade of Products. It was a combination street and county fair, first held in celebration and to promote of the new electric Red Cars, the extensive light-rail network that linked Los Angeles, Orange, Ventura, Riverside and San Bernardino counties.

With her siblings gone, Clara was left to support her mother through difficult times. But, as is often the case, by overcoming hardships she became more courageous and resilient.

DRAWING DISTRACTIONS

For Clara, drawing and painting served as a distraction from her sadness, but she also worked through her pain by escaping to the winding canyon trail near her home, with sketchbook and pencils in hand. By concentrating on drawing the rugged mountains, meandering brooks, and gentle calves grazing on their property, her problems melted away—at least for a while.

Animals were some of Clara's favorite subjects, especially their cat Huckleberry. Every day he visited the houses along the road, becoming an expert in choosing which house served the best meals. Full and satisfied after a feast of leftovers, Huckleberry would return home and curl himself into a ball, then slumber on the porch in the warm sunlight.

He was unaware that, while asleep he had become a perfect model for Clara's sketches.

"Huckleberry"

CHAPTER NINETEEN

Clara, now twenty-two, had for some time desired to expand her horizons as well as sharpen her artistic skills. She knew that this would be the perfect time to leave home for a while to focus her creative energies, continue her education, and meet new people.

Her choice? An art college in far-away New York City.

It couldn't have been easy to find a way to fulfill her dreams. The Victorian era of the late nineteenth century, was a time when most young women in Silverado, El Toro, and other California communities were expected to marry, stay home and raise a family, often starting when they were in their teens.

While Clara knew that few acceptable jobs were available to women, she also believed she could achieve whatever she put her mind to doing. And what she wanted most to do was study art.

MAKING A LIFE-CHANGING LIFE'S CHOICE

Clara had recently heard about New York City's Cooper Union. The school had been built on the dream of giving gifted, innovative minds a chance to develop their talents. Clara learned that all qualified students who were creative thinkers with a talent in art or science could receive full-tuition scholarships. Thomas Edison, inventor of the electric light bulb, had attended Cooper Union, and Clara knew that studying in an outstanding school such as Cooper Union would give her a strong foundation in art.

She applied and was soon accepted.

And Clara began packing.

Cooper Union

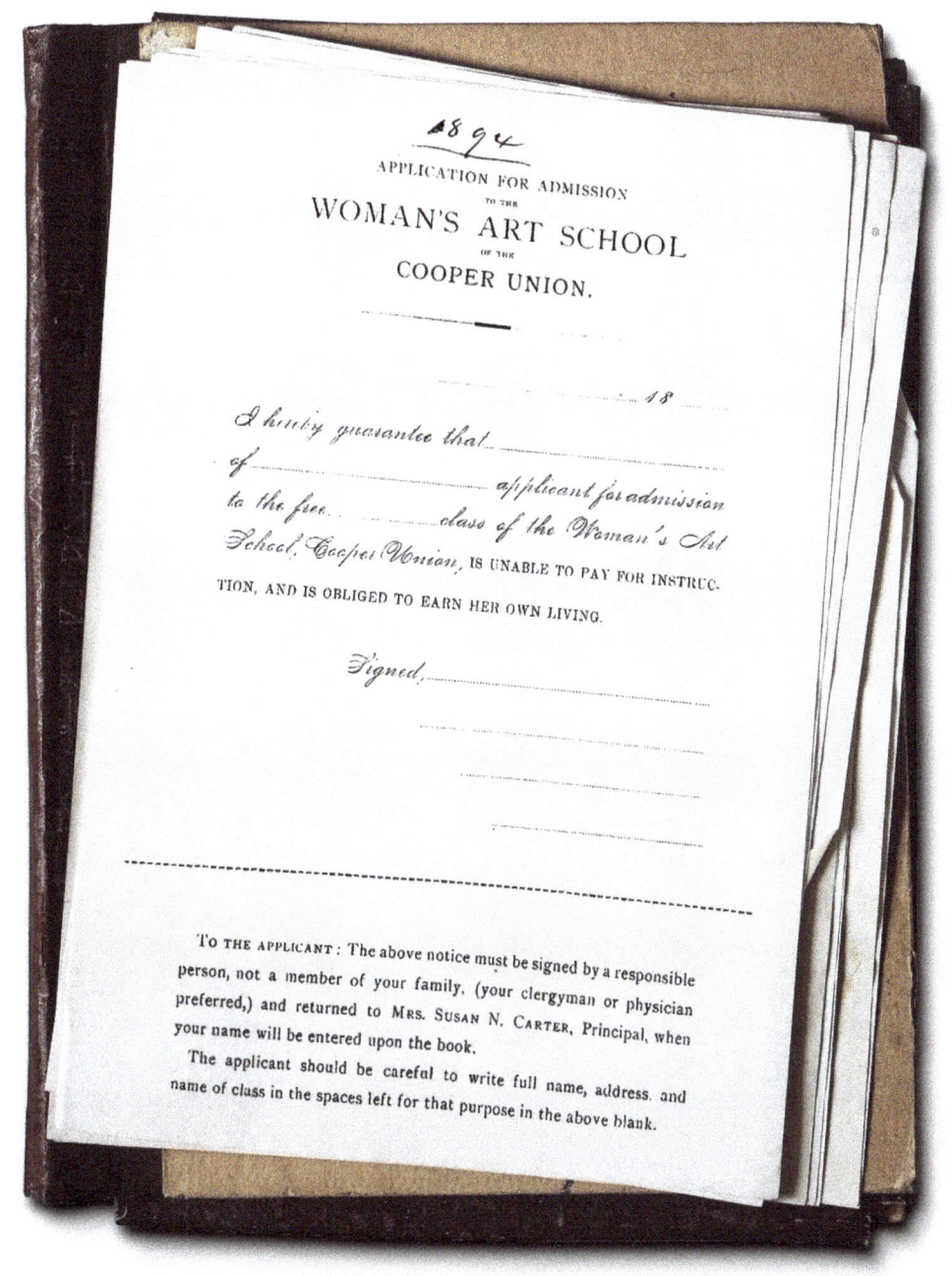

CHAPTER TWENTY

Clara's friends and family must have been astonished by the thought of this determined young woman—unmarried and unaccompanied by any male family members—traveling cross-country to New York City.

"ALL ABOARD! HEADING EAST."

In 1896, America's 3,000-mile long transcontinental railroad connecting the West and East coasts by train was one of our young nation's and the world's great achievements. And traveling from one coast to another was more than just a train ride—this was truly an exciting adventure.

At El Toro's small railroad depot, Clara boarded a northbound train to Los Angeles. After a short layover she boarded a connecting train to San Francisco, a journey of about twelve hours.

In San Francisco's Southern Pacific depot, at Townsend and 3rd. Streets she boarded yet another train. Six days after leaving El Toro she arrived in New York City. The cost was less than $90.00, or about $1,000. in today's dollars.

Clara's new life was beginning.

PART TWO

CHAPTER TWENTY-ONE

"*New York City!" The conductor announced as the train came to a hissing, shuddering halt. Clara had been anticipating arriving at New York City's impressive Grand Central Depot, since she'd left El Toro.*

Now, as she stood up to gather her things she felt the rumbling steam locomotive's great driving-wheels slowly screech and then grind to a stop as the colossal machine exhaled one last puff of hot steam.

Clara stepped off the railway car onto a vast concrete platform, then moved along with the masses of people who were making their way through America's most famous railroad depot.

Light streaming through enormous arched windows illuminating the polished marble walls, added to Clara's awe and amazement. The center of the Grand Central Depot's concourse was a vast open space that served as an elaborate entrance, welcoming visitors to New York City.

A NEW REALITY

For a moment Clara stood transfixed, her head turning from side to side.

Men with hand-held megaphones blaring out announcements for trains departing to Philadelphia, Chicago, and Boston sent passengers pressing toward their destinations.

Clara paused, confused for a moment, having never experienced swarms of rushing people like these, criss-crossing the terminal to get to their trains on time, with family and friends struggling to find and greet those who had moments before disembarked their trains.

But among all those hundreds and hundreds of people no one was waiting to welcome Clara.

FINDING HER WAY

She was alone now, detached from the comfort and security of the train and trying to find her way to the street level.

Signs pointing the way to Park Avenue and 42nd Street. She took a deep breath as she tried to decide in which direction to go.

Taking a long ramp that led up from the concourse below, Clara stopped for a few moments when she reached the street, astounded by the teeming crowds, street vendors shouting their wares, streetcar bells clanging, the overwhelming and noisy traffic of horse-drawn cabs, private carriages, freight wagons, all contributing the

clatter of horses' hooves on cobblestone.

It was an astonishing change for this pioneer girl who was accustomed to the quiet and calmness of Silverado Canyon.

LOST IN A CROWD

New York, in 1896, as it is today, was considered America's greatest city.

Exciting, alive with possibilities and a population of over one-and-a-half million, New York was without question America's most important economic and cultural center.

If Clara needed to get her mind off the Mason family's problems, New York City served as a welcomed diversion. It is known as a place where a person can get lost in a crowd or become distracted enough—at least for a while—to forget any number of troubles.

There was probably a moment when she stopped, briefly closed her eyes, took another deep breath, and—realizing she was alone and 3,000 miles away from home—hoped everything would turn out the way she had planned.

But right now she needed to find her way through this confusing maze.

Here, she quickly noticed pedestrians needed to pay attention when crossing streets. Besides the horse-drawn vehicles, shiny new electric streetcars whisked past taking passengers to destinations across town.

Horses left piles of soft manure on the pavement and Clara, used to crossing a *dirt* farmyard, now had to step carefully when crossing the *paved* street.

Beggars sat on sidewalks, hands reaching out as they pleaded with the hurrying passers-by for a few coins. Peddlers with their pushcarts called out, *"Ho, here are fresh carrots, corn, and string beans!"*

CHAPTER TWENTY-TWO

Clara made her way to the West Village, a maple tree-lined street of brownstone apartment buildings would be her new home. Perry Street was known for the many artists and poets who resided there. A flight of steps led her to a arched wooden doorway bearing the number: 62.

Clara's apartment was located on the second floor of the building, giving her a bird's eye view of the activity below.

From her tall parlor window facing Perry Street, she could look down and watch the constant motion of people. They reminded her Silverado bees moving around their hives.

On one wall was a large fireplace, and above that was a rectangular, gilded-framed mirror. In the evening, the looking glass reflected the sparkle of candles and oil lamps positioned on the fireplace mantel.

Stepping outside Clara soon discovered a lively neighborhood with art galleries, shops, and a busy stable down the street.

Passengers arriving at Perry Street by horse-drawn vehicles stepped onto a small wooden stool from their high carriages to the sidewalk. A black iron street lamp stood at the corner and illuminated the curb.

LIGHTING THE NIGHT

Each evening as the sun set, a lamplighter ignited the natural gas-illuminated lamps lining the streets one-by-one, like birthday candles on a cake. Using his ladder and a pole with a smoldering wick on the end, he reached inside the hinged doors of the lamps and lit the gas-lamp's jet.

Three thousand miles away in California, San Francisco had begun using electricity in 1879. Streetlamps, and many newer homes were conveniently illuminated by electricity. However electricity in New York was limited at the time to the business district.

Although the gas company paid him for his work, the lamplighter paid for the matches with his own money. That meant each time his wick lit a jet, he was careful to quickly close the lamp door. Otherwise, if a breeze swept by and extinguished the flame, he would have to relight a blown-out lamp using another one of his own matches.

This was truly an important job, since lamplighters also served as neighborhood watchmen on the lookout for thieves and prowlers. Then, before the sun rose over the awakening city, the lamplighters would retrace their steps, extinguishing each lamp. The quiet of dawn would be broken as rattling milk carts pulled by horses clopped their way down residential streets, delivering fresh milk to apartment occupants.

GOOD MORNING, NEW YORK CITY

In the morning, instead of the cool fresh canyon air of Silverado, Clara awoke to a mixture of city smells. The stench of manure from horse stables and odors from belching factories and breweries were layered with the perfume of flowers sold from pushcarts and wafting aromas of food cooking from nearby apartments.

On her way to school, about fourteen blocks away, Clara walked streets lined with restaurants selling delicacies she probably had never tasted, such as freshly shucked oysters from Long Island Sound, grilled flounder and halibut caught in the nearby Atlantic Ocean, and homemade pasta served with crusty Italian bread.

What a wonderful way to start the day with an omelet, warm rolls, and a hot cup of coffee at a cozy neighborhood diner—all for only ten-cents?

Immigrants who recently arrived from Italy, Hungary, and Greece, as well as many other European countries, could be heard speaking their native languages at nearby tables.

For Clara, at first all this must have been overwhelming.

In several of her early sketches we can sense her uneasiness. Like a tourist, she captured "snapshots" of her new environment through quick drawings, brief "studies" that appear to be unfinished, concentrating on simple outlines without much detail. It would take persistence, devotion to her studies, and a growing sense of comfort in her surroundings before Clara began to develop needed mastery in her artwork.

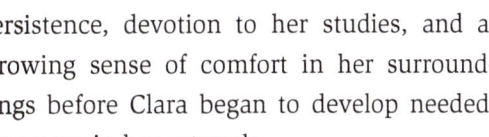

CHAPTER TWENTY-THREE

Clara now attended the Woman's Art School at Cooper Union. Classes for men and women were separate. The female student population had increased by nearly three hundred in twenty years, since more women were attending college and earning degrees. But unlike college today, only students ranging in age from sixteen to thirty-five could attend.

Cooper Union operated much like a work-study program does today. Students were encouraged to earn a living while attending school. Morning classes allowed students time in the afternoon for jobs that trained them in art-related fields of interest.

STUDYING AND WORKING AT COOPER UNION

Some of Clara's fellow students worked in advertising or as apprentices for designers. Others gave art lessons for a fee. One of the goals of Cooper Union was to bring together employers and talented students who might become their future employees.

Cooper Union stressed that "Good Character" was of equal importance for students to develop while acquiring the skills needed for success. The school was known for training students to become not only skilled artists, but responsible citizens who could make good decisions. Such characteristics were taken into consideration when recommending a pupil for a job.

Students had to work hard, and not everyone was able to complete their studies. If a pupil did not show seriousness and good effort, s/he was advised to leave the school. In fact, the period during which Clara attended Cooper Union more than five hundred students applied for the school year, but only two hundred and sixty-five were accepted.

Less than two hundred of those accepted were able to complete their coursework and eventually graduate.

SHARPENING ARTISTIC SKILLS, EARNING EXTRA DOLLARS

Clara's morning classes focused on learning to draw in pen and ink, pencil, and charcoal. Course titles included 'Drawing from the Antique,' 'Drawing from Life,' 'Perspective,' 'Cast Drawing,' 'Pen and Ink Illustration,' 'Oil Painting,' 'Crayon Photographs,' and 'Photo Color and Retouching.'

Like other Cooper Union students, Clara worked in the afternoons, probably teaching art to younger students or as an assistant to other artists, where she could use her talents as well as earn some always-needed extra spending money.

Clara, mindful of her mother's situation in California, living

without her husband, did what she could not to be a financial burden. Writing home to Mrs. Mason she explains:

"In spite of all I can do, my money goes like the wind, but any time I can, I work in the afternoons and earn my way."

MASTERING ARTISTIC SKILLS

Students listened intently to professors giving lectures on 'Design' or 'Anatomy' that focused on drawing the human form. They learned about contemporary American artists such as Mary Cassatt, France's daring new "Impressionist." Or the already renowned Claude Monet.

On Saturday evenings free art lectures were held on campus, and open to the public. Topics while Clara attended Cooper Union included *'China and the Chinese'* and *'Evolution of Society'* to satisfy the increasingly popular interests at that time in world cultures and travel.

Through practice, the guidance of her teachers, and encouragement from her classmates and friends, Clara's artistic skills reached new levels. In her 'Drawing From the Antiques' class, Clara sketched from "casts" or plaster reproductions from well-known sculptors such as Michelangelo, as well as from live models. Social custom and morals required that both statues and models remain fully clothed or draped for modesty, keeping private parts of the body "private."

New York actually seems small to me now. At first it was immense, noisy and bewildering, and I dreaded every street crossing and attempt at finding a new place. But New York is laid out so simply, police men and signs are everywhere and familiarity breeds contempt. Of course I suppose there are dangers but what you need is to keep your eyes open and tend your own business.

It is snowing now, softly but steadily. We don't intend to go to church much more until we get our spring hats and can look decent but when the weather is good for three cents we can see Jersey City, Hoboken, Brooklyn or small outlying towns.

CHAPTER TWENTY-FOUR

Clara soon joined a group of friends who quickly made up a nickname for themselves: "The Spread."

This small group of friends—Carl Bond, Polly Oliver, Cora Junks, and Ellen Freeman—soon proved to be compatible and supportive. Together, these students busily worked on school-assigned projects.

With the companionship of friends, Clara began to feel at ease in the city. It was no longer an unfamiliar place to be feared.

She frequently penned letters to her mother sharing her feelings and what was going on in her life. After a few months in the city she noted this observation:

"New York actually seems small to me now. At first it was immense, noisy and bewildering, and I dreaded every street crossing... But New York is laid out so simply, policemen and signs are everywhere..."

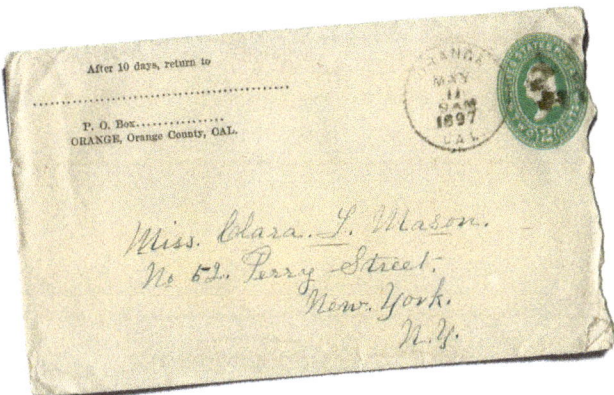

DRESSING AND IMPRESSING

Clara and her girlfriends, like most young women then and today, "dressed to impress." Hats were big, and these budding *fashionistas*, as art students like to be, must have had fun shopping together in big department stores such as Macy's and John Wanamaker & Company.

And on Sundays, they enjoyed showing off their new hats at church.

In one of her many letters to her mother, Clara noted that shops serving coffee and pie were also very popular and like Clara sketched a brief word-picture of the girls going for a quick coffee break on nearby Bleeker Street, then—on their way home—peeking between buildings for a view of the recently completed Brooklyn Bridge and a glimpse of New Jersey across the Hudson River.

Although Clara was now feeling at home in New York, able to find her way easily around the city, she also knew that with school ending, she must eventually return home to California.

CHAPTER TWENTY-FOUR 103

COOPER UNION FOR THE ADVANCEMENT OF SCIENCE AND ART.

THIRTY-EIGHTH ANNUAL COMMENCEMENT,

Saturday Evening, May 29th, 1897,

AT 8 O'CLOCK,

IN THE LARGE HALL.

TRUSTEES:

Edward Cooper, Pres't.
R. Fulton Cutting.
John E. Parsons.
Abram S. Hewitt, Sec'y.
Daniel F. Tiemann.

ADMIT GENTLEMAN AND LADIES.

Cooper Union
for the Advancement of Science and Art.

Thirty-eighth Annual Reception of the

Woman's Art School,

Thursday Evening, May 27th, 1897,
at eight o'clock.

R. Swain Gifford,
Art Director.
Mary A. Vinton,
Principal.
Abram S. Hewitt,
Secretary.

Admit Gentleman and Ladies.

CHAPTER TWENTY-FIVE

Cooper Union's school year came to an on Thursday, May 27, 1897, with the Annual Reception for the Woman's Art School.

But Clara's graduation reminded her, once again, that her parents were no longer together.

And although she had been given two tickets for them, neither of her parents would attend the ceremony. Traveling from California to New York and then turning around and returning almost immediately would have been a long journey for Nancy and George, but more importantly, the situation would have been awkward, since they were divorced.

Nevertheless, she held on to their tickets, bringing them home to California as a memento, which she placed in a box with other keepsakes.

They would not be seen again for one hundred years.

Knowing that her parents were unable to attend, Clara left for home on May 18, more than a week before the art school commencement celebration was to take place. She and her good friends, "The Spread," met together one last time at New York's

Grand Central Depot, with its tall marble columns and huge arched windows it was the perfect dramatic backdrop for their final goodbyes and presented her with a copy of Charles Dickens;s popular new novel, *Great Expectations*. Thinking of the future, Clara jotted a brief note in the book, including the time they gave it to her.

Wishing their former classmate well, "The Spread" helped Clara onboard with her baggage. Sketchbooks under one arm, and mementos in one hand they watched her as she boarded, turned and tossed them a kiss and jaunty wave. The conductor drew the open metal gate across the Pullman coach's passageway, and Clara looked back one last time.

Leaving her new friends and the city she had come to enjoy, must have been difficult. At the same time, Clara anticipated returning home to California with her developed artistic skills.

As the locomotives bell clanged again, they waved their final goodbyes.

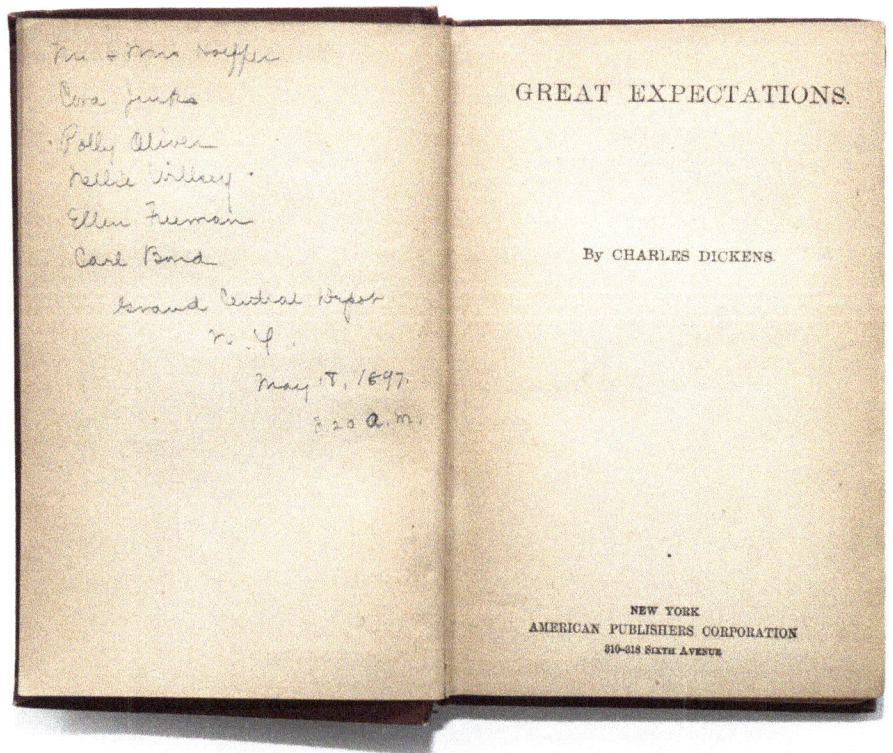

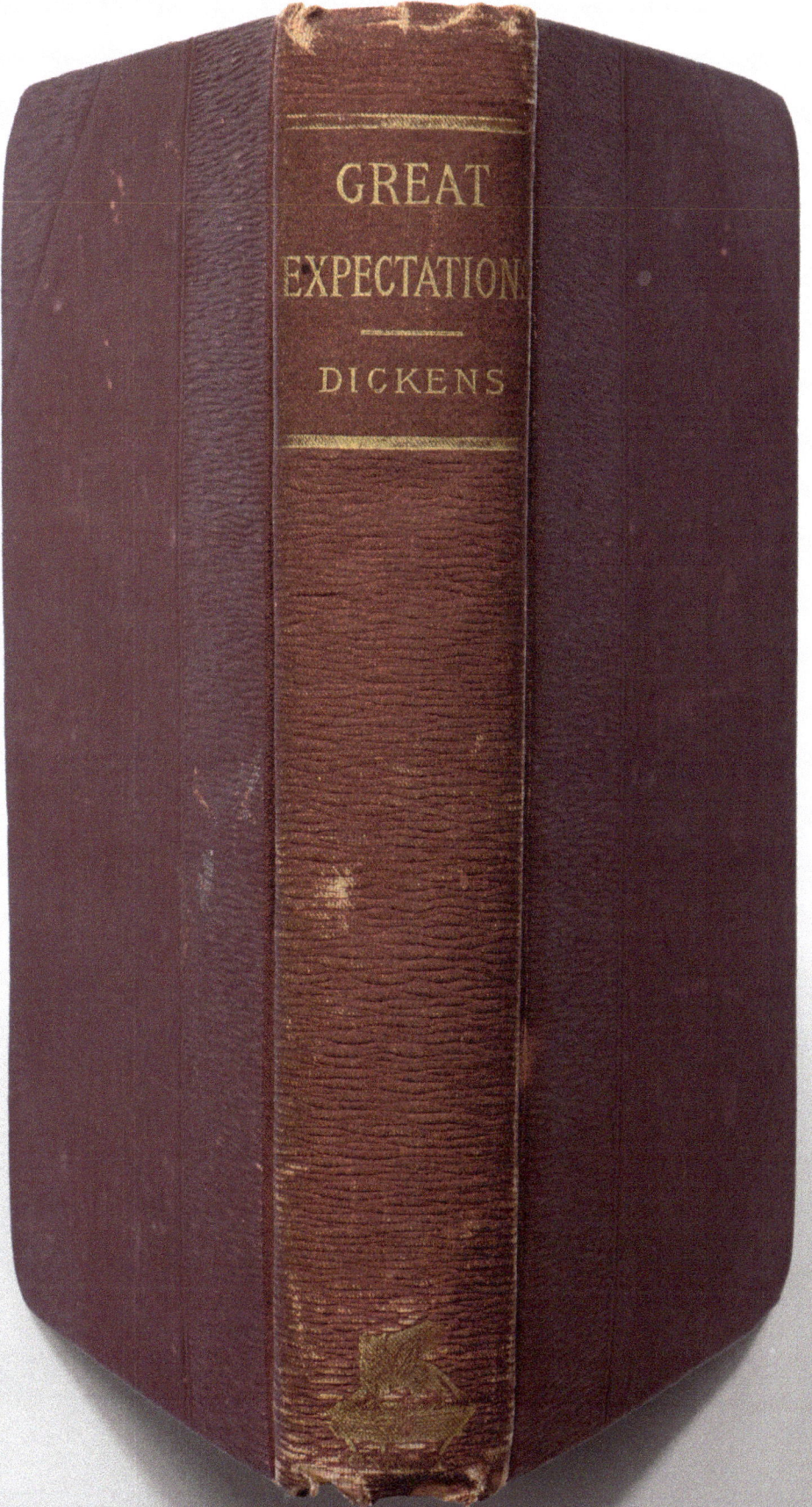

CHAPTER TWENTY-SIX

Leaning against the glass in the polished, wooden-framed window she sighed, waving last goodbyes to her friends on the platform below. Clara's locomotive was now off.

With a loud, grinding jolt, a lurch, and a series of metallic concussions, Clara fell back against her seat as the massive steel couplers mounted between the cars pulled taught, meshing, then following the big locomotive as it slowly began moving.

Clara, stood up, steadied herself, smoothed her skirt, and with a short, self-conscious glance around her, settled back into the Pullman coach's soft seat.

She took a long breath and slowly exhaled.

TRANSCONTINENTAL TRIPPER

Clara's journey traveling cross-country from New York to Los Angeles would require riding four different railroads. Two rail lines would be necessary to get from New York to Chicago. A brief layover, then her car and several others would be re-coupled to another train to Saint Louis, and then beyond the Mississippi River to Kansas City.

In Kansas she would board the Atchison, Topeka, and Santa Fe railroad, one of the five transcontinental lines that crossed the nation.

Slowly relaxing as the train gathered speed and her body adjusted to the easy, side-to-side rock'n'roll that characterizes all rail travel, she looked around at her surroundings.

PULLMAN PLUSH

This Pullman "car" as the new railway coaches were called, was a recent feature in transcontinental travel and beautifully designed for passenger comfort and privacy.

Reflecting the deep, rich tones of varnished woods such as oak, cherry, and mahogany. Dark chocolate-colored leather covered the seats. She felt secure and a little luxurious.

Passengers in Clara's coach had by now all taken their seats and were arranging items they'd brought with them for the five-day long trip. A tall man in the navy blue Conductor's uniform of the Union Pacific Railroad stopped to take her ticket.

"Ma'am," he smiled courteously, "at night, your sleeping arrangements will be provided when the car steward comes through, and in each of the car's passenger compartments, seats are converted into two comfortable beds, an upper and

a lower. You'll find the dining car three cars ahead, and our first seating for lunch will be coming up," he pulled a large railway watch with big black numbers from his vest, "at eleven. The next is at noon. I'll be stopping on my way back through to take your name for your table."

CHAPTER TWENTY-SEVEN

*ive days," Clara thought to herself as she settled back, looking out the car's window at a now-rural New York rolling by.*

This was the third long trip she'd taken by train, the first from Illinois to California with he parents when she was ten. But this new Pullman car, ten feet wide and fourteen feet tall, with a convenient bathroom was far more comfortable than the any of the others.

And now, after a year, Clara was heading home again.

But this west-bound Clara Mason who'd just a year before arrived in New York City was not the same Clara Mason.

Her studies in art, classes in sketching, composition, with her eye trained in perspective and proportion, all had contributed to a new way of seeing. And now she was aware, in that special way that artists seem to have, of how rich in subjects a simple train trip could be.

FIVE DAYS—ROLLING ACROSS THE CONTINENT

Unlike the streets of New York where people never stopped moving long enough to be easily sketched, or the rigidly posed models in her life-drawing classes who might as well have been statues, her fellow passengers were relaxed, quietly engaged in passing time, reading, playing cards, or conversing.

And they made ideal subjects for quick sketches.

She opened her new copy of *Great Expectations* "The Spread" had given her as she boarded and read the inscription.

Great Expectations—What a perfect metaphor for this trip, she thought, *and for my life as well.*

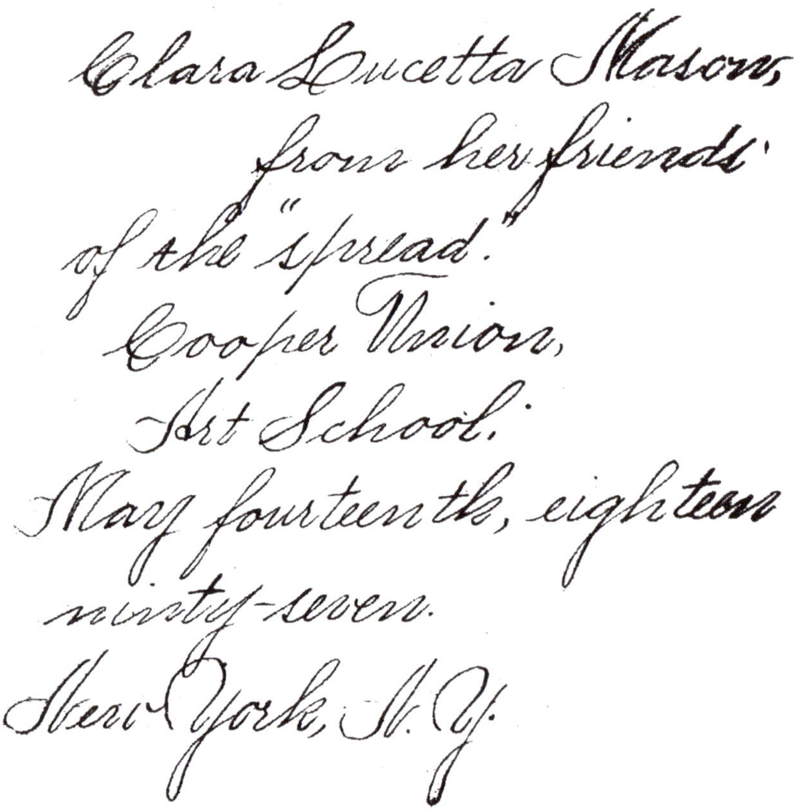

> Clara Lucetta Mason,
> from her friends
> of the "spread."
> Cooper Union,
> Art School.
> May fourteenth, eighteen
> ninety-seven.
> New York, N.Y.

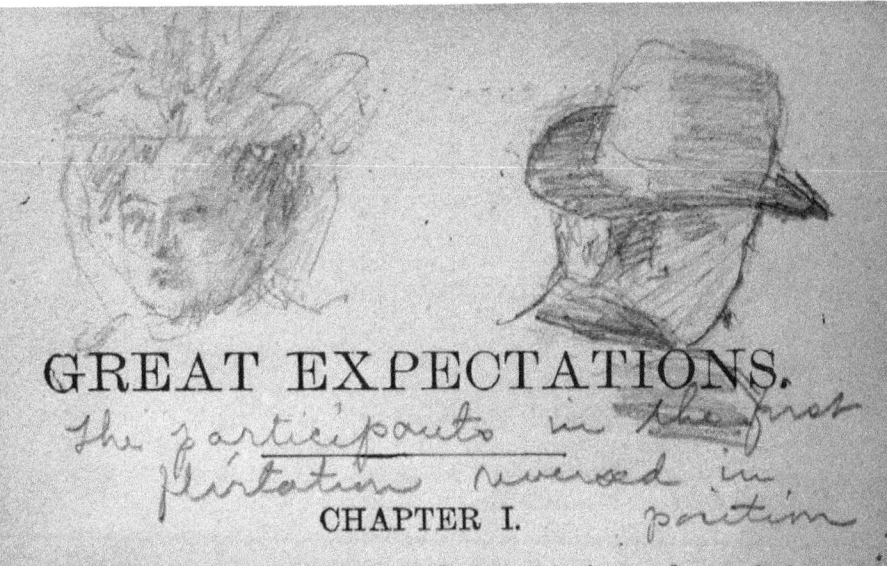

GREAT EXPECTATIONS.

The participants in the first flirtation reversed in position

CHAPTER I.

MY father's family name being Pirrip, and my christian name Philip, my infant tongue could make of both names nothing longer or more explicit than Pip. So I called myself Pip, and came to be called Pip.

I give Pirrip as my father's family name on the authority of his tombstone and my sister—Mrs. Joe Gargery, who married the blacksmith. As I never saw my father or my mother, and never saw any likeness of either of them (for their days were long before the days of photographs), my first fancies regarding what they were like were unreasonably derived from their tombstones. The shape of the letters on my father's, gave me an odd idea that he was a square, stout, dark man, with curly black hair. From the character and turn of the inscription, "*Also Georgiana Wife of the Above*," I drew a childish conclusion that my mother was freckled and sickly. To five little stone lozenges, each about a foot and a half long, which were arranged in a neat row beside their grave, and were sacred to the memory of five little brothers of mine—who gave up trying to get a living exceedingly early in that universal struggle—I am indebted for a belief I religiously entertained that they had all been born on their backs with their hands in their trousers pockets, and had never taken them out in this state of existence.

Ours was the marsh country, down by the river, within, as the river wound, twenty miles of the sea. My first most vivid and broad impression of the identity of things seems to me to have been gained on a memorable raw afternoon towards evening. At such a time I

VOL. I.   1

Carl F. Bond.

With best wishes for
a safe and pleasant
journey, from your sin-
cere friend,
May 16th 1897 Carl Franklin Bond

From upper
New York to
lower Kansas.
left us at
Kansas City.

Eye & ear
specialist,
all right
when you find
him out.

T. H. DONALD,

FIRE INSURANCE AGENT.

NEW YORK
UNDERWRITERS
AGENCY.   REDWOOD, N. Y.

"The Disagreeable Man"

Dr. C. H. Beard.
Chicago

CHAPTER TWENTY-EIGHT

Besides reading, Clara used **Great Expectations** to hold the calling cards passengers exchanged with one another as they became acquainted.

Clara drew quick sketches of passengers on Mr. Dickens's pages. Notes were jotted in pencil around the page margins describing the river valleys, open woodlands, and towns she passed. Her scribbled remarks revealed, personal insights she had about the riders on her transcontinental odyssey.

"An honest faced workman in morning clothes gazed eagerly, steadily from the window… as the train made its way to north."

As Clara's train followed along the Hudson River Valley, she made note of *"an uphill road, hedged with blooming lilacs; a little red house among the green at the top."*

Spotting a KEEP OFF THE GRASS sign in the bustling city of Albany, the capitol of New York, she noted, *"Where is the grass?"*

In Buffalo, New York, she saw the sides of huge barns used as painted billboards advertising regional products such as *Hood's Sarsaparilla* and *Warner's Safe Cure,* an over-the-counter medicine for kidney and liver ailments.

WHISTLE STOPS

At scheduled stops travelers disembarked while new riders boarded. Coach attendants assisted new passengers with their luggage and seats assignments. Often water and coal, used as fuel heat the water that created the steam to drive the locomotive's engine, was loaded right behind the locomotive in sooty black cars called "tenders."

Longer stopovers gave the continuing passengers a chance to walk around town or even find a café for a quick snack before the train departed.

CHICAGO

Reaching Chicago they were now two and a half days away from the Pacific Coast, and it offered passengers a welcome chance to stretch their legs.

At one of the longer stops past Chicago, Clara notes that she and another passenger *"…walk awhile on the streets. Find a newsboy. Make a cup of tea. Go out to the fairgrounds and cemetery. Dinner at same place, wait at depot."*

Heading back to the train, tired after their excursion, they say good night. Clara confided that she was *"in the car before it is time to go but am going straight to bed."*

CAR ART

Drawing portraits of nearby passengers gave Clara a chance to use the artistic skills she learned at Cooper Union. Along with written observations and nicknames she gave them, Clara created characters for scenarios that took place on her expedition West. There was "Mrs. Trainsick" and "The Lady of Fashion" who sat across the aisle from "Mr. and Mrs. Enthusiastic."

At one point, Clara noticed a young couple sitting across from her. *"A flirtation is progressing,"* she writes, *"(calling) cards are exchanged. He is evidently a traveling man."* It sounds like she was writing an introduction for a romance novel.

Another time, Clara spotted a mother indulging in her spoiled child's demands at lunchtime. She recorded the events.

"A luncheon occurred behind me. Daughter is treated, if she choose this or this. Fret. Fret. Two or three helpings of chicken, 2 eggs, etc. Let her eat (til) her stomach is full. Is daughter sick now? Yes!"

Soon after, Clara noted the child cried for *"…some Fletcher's Castoria,"* an old-fashioned remedy for stomachaches. The little girl discovered the hard way how too much of a good thing can make you sick.

LETTING FRED DO IT

For years railway food service was bad enough to make anyone feel like taking a tablespoon-full of Fletcher's Castoria.

By 1897, however, things had changed. Although some people might bring aboard their own food, carrying enough for five or six days wasn't either possible or practical, so reasonable meals were also available in the dining cars.

Then an entrepreneur named Fred Harvey came up with a practical solution. He built a chain of forty-seven *"Harvey House"* restaurants along the Santa Fe railroad line. Later, he added thirty specially outfitted dining cars to his operation.

Fred Harvey had quickly and surprisingly elevated the dining experience for train travelers. Recently invented refrigerated rail cars meant that delicious dinner entrees included lobster, oysters, turkey, and chicken with fresh tomato sauce could be offered. Ginger cake, prune delight, and chocolate custard made fine desserts served with sparkling silverware on white tablecloths.

Not only was the food delicious, but the servers on the trains and restaurants were a treat as well. The waitresses hired were "young women of good character, attractive, and intelligent." They became known as "Harvey Girls."

None the worse for all of this while reflecting on the scenery, Clara composed a poetic note:

> *And when our westward-speeding train*
> *Traversed the spread states of the plain*
> *That feed a world their golden grain,*
> *We climbed the mountain slopes to gain*
> *The great plateau*

BEYOND THE SANTA FE TRAIL

Snow-capped, the Colorado Rockies offered a refreshing sight after traveling several days across the flat farmlands and corn fields of Great Plains.

Clara's train pulled to a stop to offload mail and passengers and couple several new cars to the near-mile long train at Trinidad, Colorado along the old pioneers' Santa Fe Trail.

Sipping a cold Dr. Pepper under the cottonwood trees by the Purgatoire River was most refreshing.[4] Clara and a fellow-passenger joined other travelers as they sauntered along the brick streets

4. Invented in 1890, Dr. Pepper's essentially the same carbonated beverage we enjoy today.

admiring the large ornate Victorian style homes before the train whistle blew signaling passengers they would be departing soon.

On the final segment of their journey, "train agents" lumbered from car to car carrying an assortment of items in a heavy wooden box strapped around their necks. The inexpensive novelties for sale kept the adults and children amused for the last few hours of travel. Clara listed some of the items.

> *"There are: papers, magazines, confectionary sweets,*
> *fruit, curios, smelling salts, guides, soap paper, novels,*
> *dancing figurines"*

Joined by another passenger named Miss Stanfield, the two young women found that they felt sorry for the agent on their car. They thoughtfully shelled some peanuts for the poor fellow, and put them in his box which he'd left while on a break.

Unfortunately, noted Clara, *"...he doesn't know it, for the box is filled with paper (trash) when he gets it again."*

Nevertheless, it was a kind gesture from the women.

Rolling at high speed through the still-occasionally lawless desert Territories of New Mexico and Arizona, Clara knew it was a matter of hours before she would be back in California.

And she knew now, how very much she longed to see her family and friends.

CHAPTER TWENTY-NINE

*alifornia, May, 1897.* Back in Silverado, Clara stood looking out of her mother's parlor window.

Yellow bursts of Chinese lilies *"consented to bloom in the bright sunlight of spring,"* Clara's mother would note, and the bees in the apiary *"made a perfect hum as they worked strongly together,"* she added.

As if these were signs of hope, Clara felt content to be home again. Her mother welcomed Clara's companionship as well as her help, especially with the apiary. But extracting honey from the combs and delivering it to markets in Santa Ana and Anaheim was time-consuming.[5]

Clara undoubtedly looked forward to the little spare time she could find to take out her sketchbook and pencils to draw, or to sit by a creek and think about her time in New York City and what her life held in store, now that she had returned home.

The nineteenth century was coming to a close. New inventions, such as the sewing machine, telephone, and electric light

---

5. A newspaper article dated 1896 states that Clara's father George had been living further inland from Silverado, in the community of Moreno, since his divorce from Nancy.

bulb were making life easier. And these new inventions also led to new ways of thinking.

America's "New Woman" wanted more rights. Only after years of struggle, during the national movement known as Women's Suffrage, did women finally gain the legal right to vote in 1920, through the passage of the 19th Amendment to the Constitution. Women also came together to fight for better educational advantages and employment opportunities.

Clara was intelligent and a deep thinker, and she soon made a choice. Marching with a picket sign or giving speeches for women's rights was not her style. Her way of expressing her thoughts was through her creativity, artistic skills, and writing. Socially, however, she found rewards by participation in community organizations.[6]

But as most of us do, she took time for relaxation and fun. With summer coming temperatures rose into the eighties and the dry, scorching winds of Silverado blew like a blast of heat from a hot oven. Making the eighteen-mile journey west to Laguna Beach was now worth the trip.

Laguna had become a popular place for visitors from inland towns and Los Angeles. Most traveled to Laguna by way of the El Toro stagecoach.

6.Later in life, she served as secretary of her local P.E.O. (Philanthropic Educational Organization) chapter. The P.E.O. was a new organization aimed at improving educational opportunities for women that, to this day, provides scholarships and loans to further women's education. As a former teacher, Clara was well aware that a good education empowers people to succeed in the careers of their choice.

A HALF-DAY'S WAGON-RIDE TO LAGUNA BEACH

The four-hour journey to Laguna Beach began along Santiago Canyon with a turn onto the long stretch of El Toro Road.

In previous years the worst aspect of the trip was that the route was known to be a target for holdups. Sections of the road were sandy, so the horses needed to travel at a slower pace. It was along these stretches in earlier years that bandits would strike, then run for the hills. The surrounding caves that cut into the canyon walls' sandstone ledges made perfect hideouts for outlaws who would wait for the next group of unsuspecting travelers making their way down the road.

Fortunately, Clara's family always managed to get to their destination unscathed without encountering bandits.

At the end of El Toro Road, the horses turned west onto Laguna Canyon Road. Past low rolling hills, leafy sycamore and oak trees washed in golden sunlight dotted the hillsides. Where the dirt road was uneven the buggy would lurch side-to-side, twisting against the long wagon-tongue and leather "traces," and collars that bound the horses side-by-side, allowing them to evenly pull the wagon.

Occasionally the narrow country road became bumpy where parts of the road were deeply rutted after having been partially washed out, damaged during the winter's rains.

Nearing the little village of Laguna, the canyon tappered and imposing granite cliffs towered above the road which now dipped. Past outcroppings of majestic boulders they traveled, closely paralleling the sandy creek bed.

Dust kicked-up by the horses' hooves mingled with the scent of sage as they headed toward Laguna at a steady, easy trot.

CHAPTER THIRTY

As the Masons pulled into the tiny community it was now afternoon and to the West, the evening's summer sky was a watercolor wash of pink and azure streaks with violet shadows, while behind them dusk was folding across Saddleback Mountain in the east.

Laguna's tiny population swelled every June through August as visitors such as the Masons sought relief from the summer heat, and enjoyed the cool coastal breezes. Since few hotels existed in Laguna, many vacationers set up tents along the beach and cliffs.

During the last years of the nineteenth century, a lot with an ocean view could be purchased at Arch Beach on the bluff right above the sand for seventy-five dollars. For a few hundred dollars, a local carpenter would build a small house. With framed glass windows being expensive, these little "summer houses" didn't resemble today's, oceanfront homes along that same stretch at Pearl Street that take full advantage of the ocean's breezes.

Homeowners today pay millions of dollars for those same seventy-five dollar lots, with *"...whitewater and Catalina Island views"* framed through large glass sliding doors and windows.

SUN, SAND AND SEASHELLS

Laguna Beach was a place where people spent most of their time outdoors, fishing, walking along the shore, or collecting shells. Spending a day spent at the beach for girls and women meant dressing in full-length sun dresses and big bonnets to shield their faces from the sun.

For swimming, woolen swimming attire was designed more for modesty's sake than comfort, and even the lightest woolen jersey materials were heavy and soggy when wet.

Leaving the ocean, a swimmer would be forced to gather handfuls of their "bathing costume" and begin the process of wringing out what they could before toweling off. Kids just flopped in the sand making a soggy, sandy mess of themselves.

On a calm day, slight ripples on the water revealed thousands of silvery sardines below the surface. Plump lobsters were there for the taking, just a short boat row away. Drifting in a wooden skiff or bobbing buoyantly on the rolling waves were also popular pastimes on a sunny summer morning. Youngsters went barefoot as they made their way down a cliff to the beach. Fish were so plentiful they could be caught by hand in the waves and tide pools.

The Crane

ARTIST ON DECK

Clara was never far from her pencils and sketch pad while at the beach. She loved observing people and drawing even the smallest details. Her drawings give us her glimpses of what Laguna Beach's sunbathers looked like and how they dressed.

A partial eclipse.

Clara's sense of humor is obvious in her sketches of a man experiencing "a partial eclipse" under his hat and the one-legged "crane" wading into the water.

"The Arch."

Clara's beach days were devoted to collecting shells, such as iridescent abalone and tiny brown coffee shells, as she walked along the shoreline. Tide pools at "The Arch" and around Wood's Point rock formations resembled water gardens filled with swaying kelp, crabs moving like wind-up toys, and spiny sea urchins.

Afternoons at the beach were ideal for napping on the porch with refreshing ocean breezes and the rhythmic sounds of waves making a perfect way to spend a warm summer afternoon.

Clara's mother mentioned, *"The climate here at Arch Beach is the finest I ever experienced… it is seldom foggy here and not chilly cold"*

For dinner, clusters of tasty indigo-blue mussels, were gathered by the locals and boiled in big pots.

In another recollection, Clara's mother mentioned: *"At low tide we had a grand fill of abalone that were pan-fried and delicious."* Locally grown lima beans, ripe red tomatoes, and slices of sweet juicy watermelon from the Thurston family's farm, a mile south of Arch Beach, completed the meal.

CHAPTER THIRTY-ONE

*oday we forget that one hundred-plus years ago southern California was still very much a "desert coast."*

While Laguna Beach was a paradise for ocean activities, fresh water also was a real problem for its residents. Not much was available for drinking, cooking, and even washing.

A public water pump was located on Laguna Canyon Road, about two miles north of Arch Beach. Another was at Aliso Canyon, one mile south. The alternative was to purchase a barrel of water for about fifty cents from the horse-drawn water wagon that came by weekly.

ALONG THE "DESERT COAST"

Another inconvenience was the lack of indoor plumbing; outhouses were the only toilets. And without access to electricity, the dim light of candles and kerosene lanterns appeared each evening from beach cottage windows.

But for the all the inconveniences, Laguna Beach offered some unusual conveniences.

In the summertime, a butcher passed through town once a week in his wagon, providing fresh cuts of meat for the vacationers. Additionally, Laguna also had a local baker and milkman, and a barber made his rounds every two weeks, stopping at the two hotels, a sort of mobile groomer providing haircuts and shaves.

Dramatic scenery accompanied by the distinctive quality of southern California's natural light was attracting artists from as far away as the East Coast, and Europe. As one of the very first Laguna Beach artists Clara, using the poetic style of her time, was often moved to paint word-pictures in rhyme. This poetic excerpt by Clara describes the artists working at their easels along the sides of the roads.

THE LAGUNA PAINTERS

And when you pass, on either hand
The busy painters you will see;
Upon the cliffs, upon the sand,
Their wide umbrella-ed easels stand,
And there they work engrossedly.
Upon the sea with gaze intent,
Then from the range of rainbow hues
Some bits of color they will choose,
To be upon their pallets blend.

Today, artists—still inspired by *cliffs, sand, sea, and rainbow hues*—continue to paint the same vistas of the cliffs, shores, and ocean. And probably just as *"engrossedly"* as Clara's curious adverb suggests.

CHAPTER THIRTY-TWO

*esides watching the painters and locals of Laguna Beach, Clara began noticing a nearby neighbor.*

Clara had known George Fox for years. His parents were homesteaders like the Masons in nearby Bell Canyon. George's family arrived in California from Texas earlier, by wagon train on the Butterfield Stagecoach Route passing through El Paso and Fort Yuma. They too were beekeepers, aptly naming their home *Bee Ranch* and marketing their honey in Santa Ana.[7]

In the fall of 1898, George had returned home to Bell Canyon after serving as a soldier with the Seventh California Infantry in the Spanish-American War. As it turned out, the United States proved to be a world power in a war that lasted less than one hundred days. A peace treaty ended the conflict before George's unit was called into action. Thankfully, he returned home safely to both his family and his sweetheart, Clara.

George was a strong, good-looking man with a friendly smile, dark brown eyes, and thick wavy hair. His initiative and physical

---

7. Now part of the National Audubon Society's Starr Ranch Sanctuary, the one-time site of Bell Canyon's Bee Ranch is dedicated to environmental education as well as preserving rare animal habitats.

strength were necessary for the strenuous work that was available at the time. Fields and hills were being prepared for development. George and his brother were among those grading the land using mule teams and heavy equipment in areas as diverse as Newport Beach, Los Angeles, and Bakersfield. He wisely invested his income from this work in the purchase of Aliso Canyon land.

George certainly appreciated Clara's finer qualities. According to J.E. Pleasants' *History of Orange County*, teachers in Orange County were described as *"intelligent, upright, courageous, with a sense of responsibility to the community..."* —a phrase that describes Clara very well.

The couple "courted," as dating was then called, for several years. Most girls in those days were married by their late teens. But Clara was 33, the same age as George, when he asked, *"Will you marry me?"* And of course she said, *"Yes!"*

She had waited, recalling her parents' troubled marriage, until she was sure that she wanted to spend the rest of her life with her longtime sweetheart. By the time they married on June 1, 1905, in Los Angeles County, both were ready to start the next chapter of their lives together as husband and wife.

Long hours of labor in the fields gave George a good appetite when it came to Clara's cooking—hearty pot roasts, ripened tomatoes, and homemade bread with preserves. Dinner would have been served at a candlelit table near the kitchen.

After the meal they may have retreated to the parlor, playing popular songs like "Yankee Doodle" and "My Wild Irish Rose" on the little foot-pump organ. Or perhaps they went horseback riding on nearby canyon trails at dusk. Conversations might have gradually turned to the latest book Clara had read or about mutual plans for the future. Their love for each other continued to deepen. George and Clara were drawn to each other... like bees to honey.

CHAPTER THIRTY-THREE

After their marriage in 1905, Clara and George relocated wherever he could find work. Their first home was a ranch in Aliso Canyon not far from Silverado, then they moved to the growing city of Los Angeles.

George's family remained in Silverado. However, Clara's mother Nancy could no longer take care of the Silverado property by herself. Nancy sold what was left of the home's contents to move in with Clara and George.

These 1899 tax records kept at the Orange County Archives show assets from the Silverado property: furniture $30, organ $10, wagon $5, 2 horses $30, cow $15, beehives $25

Thirty-five dollars for a wagon and two horses! Today, a car can cost a thousand times that amount.

Sadly, in 1915, Clara's father died in a veterans' hospital at the age of seventy-two. Three years later, her mother passed away at the age of seventy-six. Clara mourned the loss of her parents but with George's support she moved past her grieving and into a time of great creativity.

CHAPTER THIRTY-FOUR

Once again, Clara channeled her loss and sadness into artistic energy. Her days were spent painting and writing. She created so many paintings that she generously gave them away to friends and neighbors. Today, only two of her paintings can be located.

Her first book of poetry, *In Pleasant Places*, was published in 1924. She received recognition when several of her poems appeared in the Los Angeles Times newspaper. Clara had the ability to use words and wrote with the poetic voice of that time. Here is another excerpt from her poem titled "Laguna Painters."

> *And when your coloring is done,*
> *The real painting ye have but begun.*
> *For God has worked this fair design*
> *With more than color, more than line,*
> *For he has painted, too, with wind and sun*
> *The light, the glow, and salty air,*
> *Sea-flavored: yea.*

As if Clara had not expressed herself enough through her art and poetry, she took on a new assignment: designing a house for her adored niece, Marguerite (nicknamed Marge), the daughter of Clara's sister Nellie and husband Neil McTaggert.

Since George and Clara were childless, they had a special fondness for their nephews and nieces. By the mid-1920s, Marge had married Ed Seeman, Laguna's first fire chief. Following Clara's architectural plans, their Craftsman-style home was built at 1796 Glenneyre Street in Laguna Beach, Marge and Ed raised a family and lived out their lives.

Craftsman bungalows with stone walls and clinker-brick chimneys had become a popular style of architecture in the early years of the twentieth century. Marge and Ed's house is described in the Laguna Beach City Hall land records as a "Craftsman house with box plan, multi-gabled roof and shingle siding." It had "multi-paned windows" adorning the south corner, with "an ocean stone retaining wall" extending "across the front of the lot."

Stones from the Sierra Mountains were used "to form meandering pathways" to a garden of morning glories and fragrant white freesia in back of the house. The city land record ends with this sentence: "The house was designed by Marguerite's aunt, Clara Mason Fox, artist and author of *A History of El Toro*." It was in the attic of this house that Clara's belongings were found, decades later.

CHAPTER THIRTY-FIVE

CHAPTER THIRTY-FIVE

The familiarity and charm of the Saddleback Valley lured Clara and her husband George back to the area they loved so much. In 1930, they moved again, purchasing a tract of land in El Toro (known today as Lake Forest), about ten miles from Silverado Canyon.

Earlier in their marriage, she and George had taken a six-month journey by horse and buggy to Yosemite, stopping to visit relatives along the way. The new national park in California was drawing the attention of artists, poets, and photographers.

As the couple traveled through the park they gazed in amazement at the glacial features, such as majestic El Capitan and the mighty Merced River that flowed swiftly through the Yosemite Valley. They stopped along the way and to collect unusual rocks.

Their picture-perfect house was built close to the Bennett family home. The Fox's home was similar in design to the Bennett's ranch house, with a stone fireplace and chimney. A barn stood next to

the house. Trees bearing walnuts, oranges, and plump apricots grew on the Fox property, supplying them with plenty of nuts and fresh fruit. Eucalyptus trees provided wood for their fireplace and kitchen stove.[8]

Their cow gave fresh milk and cream that was hand-churned into butter. The ample supply provided plenty for the couple and enough to share with neighbors. Dairy products were stored in a "cooler," a kind of cupboard near the cellar with wire shelves allowing the cooler air to circulate—something necessary before the days of refrigerators.

Clara added her special creative touches to the home with some unusual souvenirs collected on various trips.

NEW EXPECTATIONS AND BEGINNINGS

When it came time to build the El Toro house, Clara transformed their Yosemite rock collection along with other rocks, into a unique fireplace that served as the focal point of their living room. A stone mortar Clara had found, once used by Native Americans to grind acorns, was cemented into the fireplace as a convenient holder for matches. Her artwork decorated the walls and kitchen of the cozy Fox home.

Clara's art is notable in that she never used bright red in her landscape paintings. Her efforts focused on using muted earth tones such as azure blue, olive green, deep amethyst, and yellow ochre.

---

8. The Fox residence was located in El Toro near Cherry Street and Second Avenue. The Harvey Bennett Ranch House has been relocated to the Heritage Hill Historical Park in Lake Forest, California.

CHAPTER THIRTY-SIX

The community of El Toro in rural Saddleback Valley consisted primarily of farmers who formed a closely-knit community. Friends and neighbors helped each other in time of need, whether it was to repair a fence or help a widow harvest the year's crops. El Toro's Community Hall was the happening place for entertainment. Bonding among neighbors grew even stronger when they socialized at the Community Hall.

These gatherings were a way to say "thanks" to neighbors for helping to plant seeds or plow the hardened spring soil. One well-known ranching family, the Moultons, celebrated the end of every harvest season by hosting a dance. Community residents two-stepped well into the night by the light of kerosene lanterns as local musicians plucked bowed and their fiddles and strummed their guitars.

A surprise birthday celebration or wedding of local sweethearts also was time to celebrate. No DJs or event planners were needed for these gatherings. Loud noises from banging pots, bells, and whistles created a festive mood to announce the guests of honor before the dancing and feasting took place.

Getting dressed and ready for one of the big Community Hall dances meant extra effort. Few homes had interior plumbing and running water, so for most people a basin of water was placed on a dresser, in front of a mirror for washing and shaving. Lacking hair dryers, nail polish, or much make-up, ladies presented a more natural look and used far less "prep time" than we do today. Men and women wore their best Sunday clothes and made sure their boots and shoes were polished for the special occasion.

SOCIALIZING—EL TORO STYLE

Fun was all about spending time together with family and friends at home or at the Hall, dancing, listening to fiddle music, or sharing the latest news and gossip. As guests arrived, they proudly placed their favorite home cooked dishes on tables—savory roasts, crispy fried chicken, lima beans with butter, and black-eyed peas. Homemade frosted layer cakes and berry pies were brought for dessert.

Clara described the site for local happenings like this:

The Community Hall was the center of social life in the settlement. It was used for socials, 'school exercises,' dinners, bazaars, town meetings, and most and foremost, for country dances, held nearly always on Saturday evenings, when after a long day's work, everybody drove in from the leases and the ranches, young and old, to dance from about eight o'clock to anywhere from midnight to morning. When the children could keep awake no longer, they were wrapped snuggly in blankets and put to bed in the wagons and anterooms.

CHAPTER THIRTY-SEVEN

CHAPTER THIRTY-SEVEN

With a scarcity of water, dry farming was popular because it involved little irrigation and barley became one of the main dry-farmed crops. In her book, A History of El Toro, Clara wrote that "Dry farming is a kind of gambling," meaning a farmer could invest a lot of time and money and not get much back in return.

Clara explained a typical day for a farmhand:

Men were out of the bunkhouse by four o'clock in the morning, each tending and harnessing his own six horses or mules. Breakfast came then, and the men were out in the fields, their stock hitched to the plow by the time it was light enough to see the furrow. At noon the horses were taken from the plow, watered at the water wagon drawn to a convenient spot, and usually fed grain, occasionally hay. A wagon from camp brought the hot dinner. Table and benches were unloaded, shade rigged from the wagon with canvas, and the men sat at ease to eat. Plowing resumed, to continue to late dusk. Unhitched from the plows, each man took his team to camp, un-harnessing, feeding, and currying them before going to supper.

Late August was a busy time when the crops were ready to be harvested. Threshing machines separated the grain from the stalks. About sixteen men worked the machinery. Other workers stacked bags of grain, kept the machinery oiled, and loaded as well as unloaded the wagons. Wagon drivers called "mule skinners" brought the grain to a storage warehouse before it was shipped to cities in outlying areas. Often thirty wagons could be seen in a long line, waiting to carry in and deliver the grain. The end of the harvest was a time for the farmers to reward themselves for their hard work, providing yet another reason to celebrate at the Community Hall.

While the men were working together during harvests, club meetings provided a social gathering time for the ranchers' wives. The El Toro Women's Club helped the community by sponsoring social events such as Easter egg hunts for the children, parties, and dinners for visiting agriculturists who studied crop and soil conditions in the area. The ladies also assisted families who were struggling through hard times by providing food, clothing, and other basic necessities to make their lives easier.

A HISTORY
OF
EL TORO

by

Clara Mason Fox

CHAPTER THIRTY-EIGHT

Clara soon became a very prominent member of the El Toro Women's Club. Participation in community activities was, in fact, a priority for her. So she was pleased when, in 1938, the club asked her to write a book, which Clara titled **A History of El Toro**. As the first complete written history of the town, it had—and continues to have—great significance.

Thanks to Clara's extensive research, we can learn about the area's geographical past, its Native American heritage, the ranchero period, and the earliest days of the community. From her personal remembrances and interviews of local residents we have an idea of what life was like in the early twentieth century.

However, some topics and people were purposefully left out of her book. Interestingly, being a soft-spoken and humble woman, Clara wrote very little about herself or her own prominent pioneer family. One especially notorious murder that took place at the El Toro Community Hall was not mentioned at all.

In 1917 someone was killed due to mistaken identity. A man named Horace Munger chose to dance with a young lady. Later that night, outside the hall, her jealous boyfriend, who had eyed them dancing together, aimed and fired a gun at the man he thought was Horace. Instead, he had shot and killed an innocent man wearing a sweater similar to the one Horace was wearing.

Sadly, the deceased man had been married only a few months earlier, and his wife was expecting their first child. The murderer ran from the law and died before he was ever prosecuted.

Did Clara think this story might have marred the good reputation of her hometown, giving people the impression that El Toro was a dangerous place? Or did she decide not to bring up the issue,

knowing that it was still a sensitive subject for many El Toro residents at the time? We'll never know for sure why she omitted this story in her book.

What is easy to sense from Clara's writing is that there were aspects about country life in the early days that she yearned for, as life became more complex and modernized. Clara saw the transitions taking place in towns across the nation. She perceived one invention in particular, "the automobile," as the cause for so many changes. This new and faster method of transportation would transform small farming communities into crowded towns and even cities. history.

CHAPTER THIRTY-NINE

Clara wrote, *"Real country life is practically a thing of the past. Every family has an automobile, or two or three, and go 'to town' almost daily, so that the barber shop or lunch counter look in vain for customers, and the grocer no longer serves ranches hiring numbers of men, which in terms of horse travel, were far from other towns."*

MODERNIZATION

Clara viewed modernization as having a negative impact on relationships as well. Before the automobile, neighbors needed to depend on each other, developing stronger community ties. But now cars could transport people easily over great distances, so reliance on neighbors became less important. Clara even felt that the automobile had an impact on dating! A boy used to court and marry the girl next door, she wrote, but "now the 'girlfriend' probably lives miles away, and the boy jumps into his car, and they go to a movie or a dance at the beach."

Fortunately, Clara realized, she could preserve the simplicity and charm of small town life, as well as the natural beauty of the mountains and beaches, through her art and writings. First, she sketched the landscapes and seascapes, later using them as guides to create her paintings. Recalling her trip to Yosemite National Park with George, where years before they had traveled by horse and buggy past El Capitan and Bridalveil Falls, Clara was inspired to write poetry describing the breathtaking scenery.

> *I heard the mighty trumpets of the waterfalls:*
> *And the solemn music of many harps were*
> *The great winds in the lofty pines and the goodly cedars.*

She further created a vivid comparison of the waterfall to the clarity of glass and sheerness of fine netting.

> *...They were carved as of glass;*
> *They were spread with veils.*

SOCIAL CHANGE

Her dismay about social changes, however, didn't mean Clara rebelled against all modern conveniences. Soon after moving to El Toro, she became the proud owner of a new invention: the washing machine. This innovative device consisted of a wooden tub with a hand-operated wringer. There were, however, still no clothes dryers. Instead, clothes were hung on a clothesline to dry in the fresh air. And like everyone else, Clara and George eventually traded in their horse and buggy for an automobile.

Reluctantly, they knew they must.

CHAPTER FORTY

In 1931 George's brother Frank and his family decided to settle in El Toro to live closer to their relatives. Frank and his wife Florence had a nine-year-old daughter named Gwendoline. Gwen is one of the last living relatives who remembers Clara and George.

Of course, I wanted to meet Gwen to hear stories about her Aunt Clara and Uncle George. In 2011, my husband and I made a trip to visit Gwen and her husband Boyd in their hometown of Loveland, Colorado.

Gwen still holds precious a gift from Uncle George and Aunt Clara—her first Bible. It was personalized with "GWEN" engraved in gold on the cover. Bible as a cherished remembrance of her aunt and uncle.

Gwen as well as former residents of El Toro remembered Clara and George as kind and good-hearted neighbors who went out of their way to help others. Some recall holiday seasons when generous-sized cartons filled with fruit, homemade preserves, fresh vegetables, and fried chicken were graciously given from the Fox household.

WAR EFFORT REPLACES AGRICULTURE

On December 7, 1941 the Japanese attacked Pearl Harbor, Oahu, prompting the United States to enter World War II. That meant workers were needed to build planes, weapons, and other equipment for our military. Women became a larger part of the work force as men went off to war. A training station for the Marines was built near El Toro, employing many local workers.

UNITED STATES OF AMERICA

War Ration Book One

WARNING

1 Punishments ranging as high as *Ten Years' Imprisonment or $10,000 Fine, or Both,* may be imposed under United States Statutes for violations thereof arising out of infractions of Rationing Orders and Regulations.

2 This book must not be transferred. It must be held and used only by or on behalf of the person to whom it has been issued, and anyone presenting it thereby represents to the Office of Price Administration, an agency of the United States Government, that it is being so held and so used. For any misuse of this book it may be taken from the holder by the Office of Price Administration.

3 In the event either of the departure from the United States of the person to whom this book is issued, or his or her death, the book must be surrendered in accordance with the Regulations.

4 Any person finding a lost book must deliver it promptly to the nearest Ration Board.

OFFICE OF PRICE ADMINISTRATION

№ 305323 -35

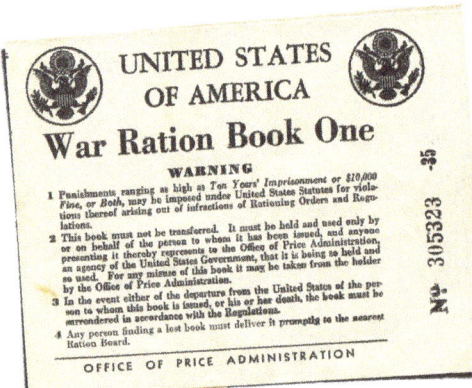

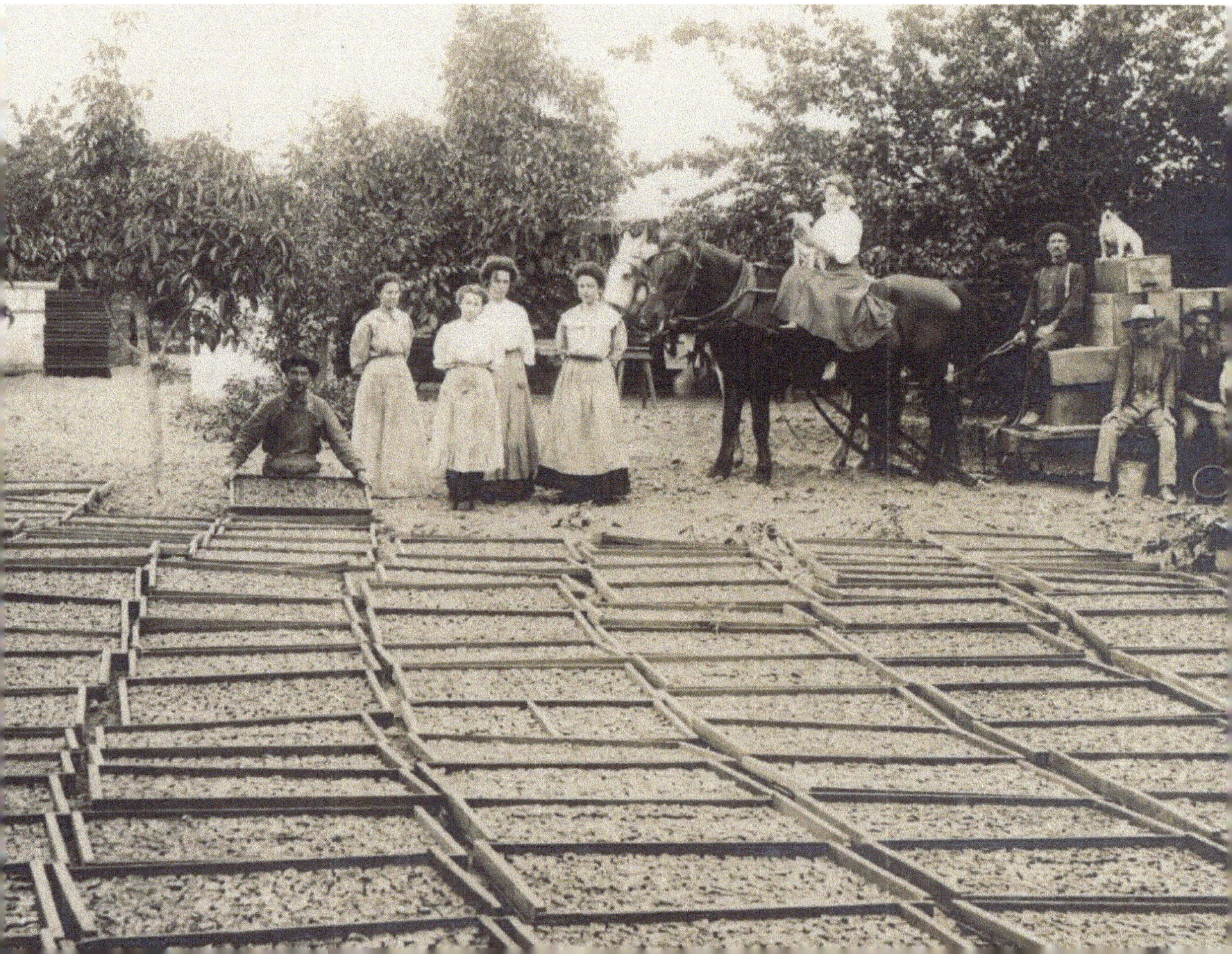

When the war ended victoriously in 1945, soldiers returned home to marry and start families. A number of servicemen who had

been stationed at the El Toro Marine Corps Air Station decided to return and settle Orange County. Along with a growing population and greater demand for goods and services, further transformation in towns and cities began to take place. Fewer people patronized the old-fashioned general stores to purchase food items from their limited variety of local farm products. A new kind of store, the "supermarket," carried larger choices of meats, fruits, and vegetables, often shipped in from around the country. A web of highways now connected cities across the nation.

While much of Orange County was growing and expanding, Laguna Beach remained a quiet beach community in Orange County. When the upkeep of their El Toro property became too much for them, Clara and George moved back to Laguna Beach. A short time afterwards they relocated to the inland town of Tustin where George passed away in 1951 at the age of 77.

Receiving full military honors for his service in the Spanish-American War, remaining soldiers from his Infantry unit stood at attention by his grave, dressed in military uniforms to pay final respects to their old comrade. As George's casket was slowly lowered into the ground at his family gravesite in Santa Ana, a former soldier solemnly played the traditional "Taps" on his trumpet. Clara said her final good bye to the man she loved.

Clara returned to Laguna Beach to live near her niece, Marge and her family.

As predicted by the woman who wrote the history of El Toro, the once rural community has gone through changes, including its name. Lake Forest, as it is known today, is a city with modern shopping centers, rows of tract homes, and wide, well-lit streets.

When Clara was young she traveled along dusty country roads on horseback. By the end of her life in 1959, she had witnessed the dawn of the Space Age with exploration into outer space in rockets. How much the world had changed.

Clara Mason Fox passed away on March 11, 1959 at the age of 85. She is buried next to her devoted husband George at the Santa Ana Cemetery in Santa Ana, California.

Packed away in Grandma Marge's attic, her memories were forgotten for many years, until being discovered by a new generation.

Eriogonum

Plant — 5-12 ft. high. annual.
Stems — not woody. Pithy, erect.
Leaves — Radical. Apparently spatulate.
Inflorescence — Compound umbel. Three-bracted. Bracts
    sharp + strong, large flower in axil.
Calyx — Am not sure if the apparent petals & sepals + apparent
    sepals bracts. If calyx is the brown, then it is tubular, with
    three acuminate lobes. Brown.
Corolla — Salverform, rose red, 6 lobes.
Stamens — Apparently nine. Extended beyond corolla
    tube, + inserted on its base.
Pistil — One, two long filiform styles.
Fruit —

    Sheathing stipule at joints of the stem.
    Friend Ranch, South hill side.

        Family — Polygonaceae (?)
        Genus — Eriogonum.

CHAPTER FORTY-ONE

Something unexpected happened while I was writing this book. I received an email from a friend, journalist Janet Whitcomb, saying she had come across a press release published by the Rancho Santa Ana Botanic Garden (RSABG) about Clara Mason Fox.

In 2010, a number of illustrations were found filed with actual plant specimens in their Herbarium. Although they were detailed watercolors paintings depicting a variety of wildflowers found in Orange County, they could not be used as actual plant specimens for study. So they were brought to the archives where they were recorded and stored. With the earliest ones dated 1894, they were protected in the dark drawers for years. The colors retained their brilliance. The artist who created the watercolor illustrations was Clara Mason Fox.

AN ADDITIONAL DISCOVERY

Comparing Clara's earlier pencil drawings to her vibrant watercolor paintings is like looking at a black-and-white photo next to a vivid HD image. The pastel and jewel-toned colors look amazingly lifelike and intense, as though they recently had been painted. Delicate flowers with stamens and bristly leaves give the paintings a three-dimensional quality. Some illustrations include hand written botanical descriptions. Others look like works in progress showing light pencil outlines.

To date, more than one hundred fifty have been found. Each had been stamped with a number so they know approximately seven are yet to be found. The Herbarium has more than a million specimens stored in their cabinets, so until researchers come across the paintings by chance, they will remain concealed.

Jessica Dewberry, the 2010 *Getty Multicultural Undergraduate Intern*, was assigned to research the paintings for accuracy and digitize the images. She became intrigued with the artist who had created the mini-masterpieces. She wondered, *Who was Clara Mason Fox?* Jessica searched for biographical information but could find only references to Clara's birth, death, and that she had been inspired by the beauty of Silverado Canyon. My husband and I met with Jessica and other researchers at the RSAGB library to provide the details we knew about Clara's life. They were amazed to hear about Clara's other achievements as a teacher, poet, and author.

We were pleased to learn that the watercolors were deemed to be of such artistic importance that the Huntington Library in San Marino, California decided to show the paintings along with other well-known botanical painters in an exhibit called *"When They Were Wild:* Recapturing California's Wildflower Heritage."

One of the most recent discoveries has been a seascape painting found in a closet where it was stored for twenty-five years. Coated with several layers of varnish and grime, the oil painting was carefully restored to its original radiance. The calm phosphorescent waters of Laguna Beach stretch toward the seashell-pink horizon in this small-sized oil painting with Clara's signature written in pencil.

Rescued from obscurity, Clara's life and accomplishments are being rediscovered and illuminated for all to recognize and appreciate. As she continues to reveal herself through her art and writings, I wonder what future discoveries about Clara Mason Fox might be found.

Clara's story, which is truly that of a multi-faceted woman, a California pioneer, a teacher, a poet and an artist, offers inspiration. We can learn as Clara's example proves how to take problems and challenges in our own lives and use them to help us become stronger and more resilient individuals. Even if we can't all design a Laguna Beach house or write a history book, perhaps Clara's example will help you find your own strengths to express the things that matter to you.

THE LIFE OF

Moves to Silverado Canyon, Orange County
1887

Marries George Fox
1905

Masons farm in Illinois
1880

Studies art at Cooper Union in NYC
1896–1897

Born to George & Nancy Mason in Ohio
November 24, 1873

Begins teaching in Silverado Canyon
1891

1870 1875 1880 1885 1890 1895 1900 1905 1910 1915 192

Ulysses S. Grant is President
1869–1873

Santa Fe Railroad extends to Orange County
1887

Thomas Edison invents the light bulb
1879

Spanish-American War
1898

WWI
1914–1918

Oil discovered in Los Angeles
1892

19th Amendment gives women the right to vote
1920

WORLD

CLARA MASON FOX

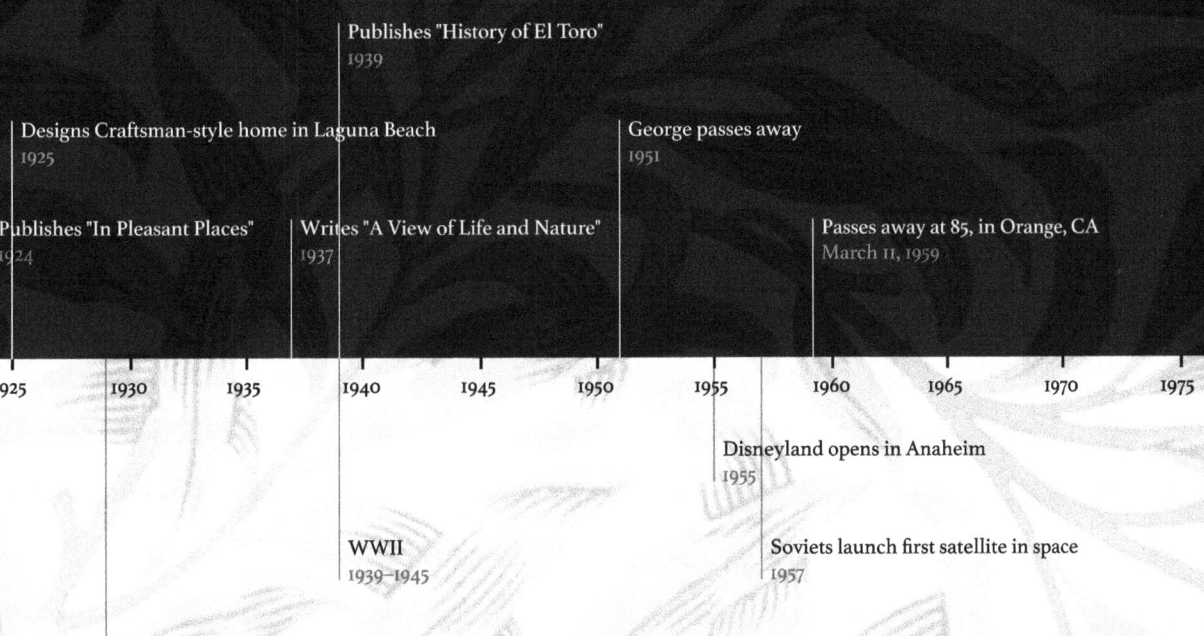

Publishes "History of El Toro"
1939

Designs Craftsman-style home in Laguna Beach
1925

George passes away
1951

Publishes "In Pleasant Places"
1924

Writes "A View of Life and Nature"
1937

Passes away at 85, in Orange, CA
March 11, 1959

1925 1930 1935 1940 1945 1950 1955 1960 1965 1970 1975

Disneyland opens in Anaheim
1955

WWII
1939–1945

Soviets launch first satellite in space
1957

The Great Depression
1929–1939

EVENTS

IN PLEASANT PLACES
BY
CLARA MASON FOX

POEMS FROM "IN PLEASANT PLACES"

by Clara Mason Fox

A CONTRAST

The sunlight glitters coldly on the snow
That robes the mountain slopes and weights the pine
Whose rich greens show the darker. Crystalline
The chill air hangs, and still. But see! Below,
A sun-steeped valley glimmers in a show
Of color—a wide mosaic whose design
Is laid in squares of green, with interline
Of white—the thread-like roads that come and go.
Among the orange-groves and grain-fields wind
The streams, like silver ribbons, to the sea
Whose level blue at the horizon lies,
Dimmed in blue haze. A contrast sharp-defined!
Here—winter and the calendar agree,
And there—dwells summer as of Paradise!
February—

ARCH BEACH

Bright golden headlands stepping in the sea,
Fretted by age-long strife of wind and wave
In spanning arch and glooming, yawning cave,
Where still the green waves battle furiously;
Far sea and sky one blue profundity,
And outer sapphire, inner emerald pave
The ocean floor; the breakers, thundering, lave
Each curving beach in foaming bravery,—
A fringe of white to mark the sea's purlieu.
I can but trust that in another plane
Of being, we shall have sensations new
And keener,
Know a fuller life of bliss,
But I've no guess of what I could attain
Of greater joy or beauty than just this.
August—

THE LAGUNA PAINTERS

A range of hills here marks the changing shore
Of a deep sea whose lucent waters run
In splendid colors to its cliffs of dun
And tawny gold. Here lies the watery floor
In glorious greens, and purples, blue at fore
To distant indigo. Each turn is won
A picture new and each more perfect seeming.
The jutting headlands, golden-beaming,
Are planted in the sea, whose green tide lift
And throw themselves in spray white-gleaming
Upon the rocky slopes, and, backward streaming,
Pour whitening to the coming waves, the drift
Of seaweed left in wreaths in every rift
Or cleft of rock, where wind and wave
Have fretted gargoyles, cornice, peristyles;

And they have cut off little golden isles
And black and rugged rocks, all honeycombed and eaten;
Or long, low hedges that still forward creep
Onto the deeper sea, where o'er them sweep
The heaving swells, that, mangled, foaming, beaten,
A whitened smother show upon the emerald deep.
Between the points lie little crescent beaches,
Curves of palely-gleaming sand,
And o'er the opalescent shallower reaches
The swells come surging strongly toward the land,
They tower, and greenly break, and on the strand
They fling their lacy scallops.
Wind and ocean
Are mingling in wild commotion.
The waters crash upon the rocky wall,
With thundering roar the breakers fall;
They brawl in forward rushing motion,
To sink away into a heaving sigh;
Then o'er they sand they whisper, lisp,
Returning wavelets curling crisp
Above the rippling sands they lave.
The little wading sea-birds cry,
So plaintive-sweet, and, sweeping by
The wind goes roaring through his rocky caves.
But not one sound we hear alone,
For all are mingled with the deep, sad tone,
The voice of the unresting waves,-
Are merged into a monotone
Of grief. But yet, the sadness and the sound
Are but the hem upon the outer bound
Of that vast drapery
Of calm and silence, deep, profound,
That wraps the sleeping sea;
The restless movement but the bright embroidery
Wrought by the winds on the eternal peace that broods
Upon the watery solitudes.

And when you pass, on either hand
The busy painters you will see;
Upon the cliffs, upon the sand,
Their wide-umbrellaed easels stand,
And there they work engrossedly.
Upon the sea with gaze intent,
Then from the range of rainbow hues
Some bits of color they will choose,
To be upon their palettes blent.

With head drawn back, and eyes half-closed,
The strokes of color are disposed
Upon the waiting canvas—then
Upon the sea they gaze again.
O busy painters, what can ye do?
If your gods be kind, and ye be true,
With your pastes of ore, and your bits of clay
The rounded hills ye might build anew,
With yellow ochre these cliffs portray;
Your madder, gamboge, indigo
Again be made to live and grow
In gray-green brush on their fair plateau.
But what of the wonder of the sea?
Can mauve or cobalt blue, or green,
Can iron, copper, zinc, or lead
Dead chrome or sodium, ultramarine,
Depict this lucid ocean bed?
A palette of gems ye would require
This limpid floor would ye inlay—
Amethyst, emerald, deep sapphire,
And chips of diamond, sparkling fire,
To sprinkle o'er; the milky play
Of opal here these shallows display.

And when your coloring is done,

The real painting ye have but begun.
For God has worked this fair design
With more than color, more than line,
For He has painted, too, with wind and sun
The light, the glow, the salty air,
Sea-flavored; yea, and He has painted there
With ceaseless movement and unending sound;
Has wrought relief of glittering strife upon a ground
Of still blue peace.
Can ye ensnare
In paint the movement on the beaches?
Can ye add the thunder, or the moan and sigh,
The salty-tang, the sea-bird's cry?
Can ye paint the lure of the indigo reaches,
That, when the eye would rest, beseeches,
And draws it on and on unendingly?
From what dull tube can ye express
The peace that lies upon this sea?
Can ye show rest in strife, in power, tenderness?
Or paint this thought of God and of eternity?
Yea, He has set a model there
To drive a struggling painter to despair;
To lure him on with stretches vast,
With thousand pictures, color fair,
And then to humble him at last.
But he may think he has done much
If in his study he shall bring
Away with him the faintest touch
Of beauty thus divine, of this rare coloring,
Some hint of feeling to his canvas cling.
And surely, sitting there, alone,
In stillness, working patiently,
There shall be something in the waves' deep tone
Will speak to him; some of the beauty of the sea
Pass in his soul; some of its peace become his own,
Some of its power, its sublimity.

RESOURCES

"American History Timeline 1780-2005." www.Animatedatlas.com.

"American Memory." Amtrak, Library of Congress, http://www.loc.gov.

Boehle, Richard. "Blizzard of 1888." http://www.vny.cuny.edu/blizzard.

California Census Records. 1900, 1910, 1920, 1930. National Archives.

Cooper Union Annual Reports, May 29, 1896 and May 29, 1897.

Cooper Union Women's Art School Book of Rules and Regulations. ca. 1885-87.

"Craftsman Bungalow House Style." http://architecture.about.com.

"Discovery of Oil in Los Angeles." http//www.usc.edu/libraries/archives/la/oil.html.

Ellis, Harry E. "Disneyland's History." http://www.justdisney.com/disneyland/history.html.

"Soft-Drink Industry." http://online.org/tsha

Fox, Clara Mason. A History of El Toro. Lake Forest, California: El Toro Woman's Club, 1938.

Fox, Clara Mason. A View of Life and Nature: Poems. El Toro, California: Unpublished Mimeographed Document, 1937-1938.

Fox, Clara Mason. In Pleasant Places. Los Angeles, California, Grafton Publishing Corporation, 1924.

"Frontier Trails of the Old West." http://www.frontiertrails.com/butterfield htm.

"The Homestead Act." http://www.nps.gov/archive/home/homestead_act.html.

Illinois Census Records. 1880. National Archives.

Johnson, Gwendoline and Boyd. The John Syndol Fox and Margaret Elizabeth Spear Story. Loveland, Colorado: Unpublished Document, 2005.

"Lamplighters of Olde Middle Village." www.junipercivic.com/.

"Lincoln's Cooper Union Address Propelled Him to the White House." Robert McNamara, http://About.com.

McClelland, Elsie. Silverado Canyon Sketches: 1853-1953. Historical Society of Southern California, 1957.

Miller, Ilana, "The Victorian Era." http://victoriaspast.com.

Naylor, Natalie N. (editor). Journeys on Old Long Island. Interlaken, New York: Empire State Books, 2002.

"New Mexico's History." www.nmartmuseum.org/nmhistory.html.

"Orange County Great Park." http://www.ocgp.org/learn/history.

Orange County Historical Commission. A Hundred Years of Yesterdays. Orange County, California: Orange County Historical Commission, 2004.

Osterman, Joe. The Old El Toro Reader: A Guide to the Past. Whittier, California: Old El Toro Press, 1992. ibid. Stories of Saddleback Valley. Whittier, California: Old El Toro Press, 1992.

Payne, Theodore. Theodore Payne in His Own Words. Pasadena, California: Many Moon Press, 2004.

Pleasants, J.E. History of Orange County. Los Angeles, California: J.R. Fennell and Sons, 1931.

Ramsey, Merle and Mabel. Pioneer Days of Laguna Beach. Laguna Beach, California, Mission Printing Company, 1967.

Silverado Files. BX3/30, Silverado Public Library. Silverado, California.

Valentino, Thomas. "Farming in Young Illinois." www.lib.niu.edu/2000.

"Women's History in America." http://www.wic.org.

"World Events." http:// www.infoplease.com.

"Yosemite." www.nps.com.

INTERVIEWS

Barrios, Russ. Pitcher Park Docent, Beekeeping in Orange County, Orange, CA, September 9, 2011.

Johnson, Gwendoline and Boyd, George and Clara Fox's niece and husband, Loveland, CO. August 1, 2009, August 9, 2011.

Whitcomb, Janet. Modjeska House and Gardens Docent, County of Orange Historical Parks, February 11, 2012.

PHOTO INDEX

6 .... Marge and Ed Seeman's house on Glenneyre Street

10 .... 1896 sketch of Clara's mother completed in one hour

11 .... Our daughter Inaeko in the same rocker (1984)

16 .... Christian Sunday School

18 .... Clara at one year old

30 .... Clara with her dad

32 .... (Left to right) George, Nellie, Nancy, Charley and Clara

34 .... Nellie with her father. He's wearing a G.A.R. medal (Courtesy of the Sons of Union Veterans of the Civil War)

39 .... Santa Fe Depot, Santa Ana, 1911 (Photo courtesy Orange County Archives)

40 .... Orange County in 1897 (Courtesy of the Orange County Archives)

50-51 .... The Mason Family's Silverado Canyon home

54-55 ...... Campers in the Canyon (Courtesy of First American Corporation)

56 .... La Mode Illustrée-p.241,1887 (Public Domain: authors life plus 70 years)

58 .... 1902 - Charles Dana Gibson's "Studies in expression. When women are jurors." (Public Domain: published before 1923)

59 .... Clara at fifteen years old

62 .... Clara at nineteen years old

68 .... Theodore Payne (Courtesy of Theodore Payne Foundation for Wild Flowers and Native Plants)

72 .... Clara's mother

74 .... Clara's sketch of the apiary and extracting house

76 .... Neil McTaggart

78 ....(Back row, standing) brother-in-law Neil McTaggart and 21 year old Clara. (Front row) Clara's sister Nellie with her son Raymond (age 5) and Ralph (age 3) next to Clara's mother, holding 5-month-old Marguerite (Marge) on her lap.

80 ....Clara in her early twenties

83 ....Application for Admission (Courtesy of Cooper Union Archives Library)

84 ....Old El Toro Train Station by Saddleback Valley

89 ....1890s New York City Map (PD-US)

122 ....Horse-drawn Stagecoach in Laguna Canyon in 1898 (Courtesy of Bowers Museum)

124 ....Oil painting by Clara Mason Fox of Saddleback Valley (ourtesy of Brad Smith)

126 ....Watercolor of John J. Seeman's house at Arch Beach painted by Mary F. Bradshaw.

128 ....Wading in a Laguna tide pool, 1899 (Courtesy of Bowers Museum)

129 ....Laguna Beach bathers c. 1809s (Courtesy of Bowers Museum)

131 ....Arch Beach in the late 1800s (Courtesy of First American Corporation)

134 ....Forest Avenue, Laguna Beach early 1900's (Laguna Beach Historical Society)

138 ....George and Clara

142 ....George, Clara's mother Nancy and Clara at the El Toro house.

147 ....1796 Glenneyre Street, Laguna Beach

152 ....El Toro Community Hall (Courtesy of the Heritage Hill Historical Society)

169 ....Holy Bible given to Gwen Fox by Clara and George Fox

171 ....El Toro General Store Area (Courtesy of Bowers Museum)

173-177 ...Botanical Watercolors by Clara Mason Fox (Reproduced with the permission of the Archives of Rancho Santa Ana Botanic Garden, Claremont, CA)

www.ingramcontent.com/pod-product-compliance
Lightning Source LLC
Chambersburg PA
CBHW061118010526
44112CB00024B/2907